W9-AVO-142

COMPUTER ANIMATION

by Hal Marcovitz

LUCENT BOOKS

An imprint of Thomson Gale, a part of The Thomson Corporation

THOMSON

GALE

Detroit • New York • San Francisco • New Haven, Conn. • Waterville, Maine • London

THOMSON

✳ ™

GALE

For more information, contact
Lucent Books
27500 Drake Rd.
Farmington Hills, MI 48331-3535
Or you can visit our Internet site at http://www.gale.com

LIBRARY OF CONGRESS CATALOGING-IN-PUBLICATION DATA

Marcovitz, Hal–
Computer animation / by Hal Marcovitz.
    p. cm. -- (Eye on art)
Includes bibliographical references and index.
ISBN 978-1-4205-0004-2 (hardcover)
1. Computer animation—Juvenile literature. 2. Cinematography—Special effects—
Juvenile literature. 3. Digital cinematography—Juvenile literature. I. Title.
TR897.7.N37 2008
006.6'96—dc22

                                                                2007022928

ISBN-10: 1-4205-0004-X
Printed in the United States of America

CONTENTS

Foreword

"Art has no other purpose than to brush aside . . . everything that veils reality from us in order to bring us face to face with reality itself."

—French philosopher Henri-Louis Bergson

Some thirty-one thousand years ago, early humans painted strikingly sophisticated images of horses, bison, rhinoceroses, bears, and other animals on the walls of a cave in southern France. The meaning of these elaborate pictures is unknown, although some experts speculate that they held ceremonial significance. Regardless of their intended purpose, the Chauvet-Pont-d'Arc cave paintings represent some of the first known expressions of the artistic impulse.

From the Paleolithic era to the present day, human beings have continued to create works of visual art. Artists have developed painting, drawing, sculpture, engraving, and many other techniques to produce visual representations of landscapes, the human form, religious and historical events, and countless other subjects. The artistic impulse also finds expression in glass, jewelry, and new forms inspired by new technology. Indeed, judging by humanity's prolific artistic output throughout history, one must conclude that the compulsion to produce art is an inherent aspect of being human, and the results are among humanity's greatest cultural achievements: masterpieces such as the architectural marvels of ancient Greece, Michelangelo's perfectly rendered statue *David*, Vincent van Gogh's visionary painting *Starry Night*, and endless other treasures.

The creative impulse serves many purposes for society. At its most basic level, art is a form of entertainment or the means for a satisfying or pleasant aesthetic experience. But art's true power lies not in its potential to entertain and delight but in its ability to enlighten, to reveal the truth, and by doing so to uplift the human spirit and transform the human race.

One of the primary functions of art has been to serve religion. For most of Western history, for example, artists were paid by the church to produce works with religious themes and subjects. Art was thus a tool to help human beings transcend mundane, secular reality and achieve spiritual enlightenment. One of the best-known, and largest-scale, examples of Christian religious art is the Sistine Chapel in the Vatican in Rome. In 1508 Pope Julius II commissioned Italian Renaissance artist Michelangelo to paint the chapel's vaulted ceiling, an area of 640 square yards (535 sq. m). Michelangelo spent four years on scaffolding, his neck craned, creating a panoramic fresco of some three hundred human figures. His paintings depict Old Testament prophets and heroes, sibyls of Greek mythology, and nine scenes from the Book of Genesis, including the Creation of Adam, the Fall of Adam and Eve from the Garden of Eden, and the Flood. The ceiling of the Sistine Chapel is considered one of the greatest works of Western art and has inspired the awe of countless Christian pilgrims and other religious seekers. As eighteenth-century German poet and author Johann Wolfgang von Goethe wrote, "Until you have seen this Sistine Chapel, you can have no adequate conception of what man is capable of."

In addition to inspiring religious fervor, art can serve as a force for social change. Artists are among the visionaries of any culture. As such, they often perceive injustice and wrongdoing and confront others by reflecting what they see in their work. One classic example of art as social commentary was created in May 1937, during the brutal Spanish civil war. On May 1 Spanish artist Pablo Picasso learned of the recent attack on the small Basque village of Guernica by German airplanes allied with fascist forces led by Francisco Franco. The German pilots had used the village for target practice, a three-hour bombing that killed sixteen hundred civilians. Picasso, living in Paris, channeled his outrage over the massacre into his painting *Guernica,* a black, white, and gray mural that depicts dismembered animals and fractured human figures whose faces are contorted in agonized expressions. Initially, critics and the public condemned the painting as an incoherent hodgepodge, but the work soon came to be seen as a powerful antiwar statement and remains an iconic symbol of the violence and terror that dominated world events during the remainder of the twentieth century.

The impulse to create art—whether painting animals with crude pigments on a cave wall, sculpting a human form from marble, or commemorating human tragedy in a mural—thus serves many purposes. It offers an entertaining diversion, nourishes the imagination and the spirit, decorates and beautifies the world, and chronicles the age. But underlying all these functions is the desire to reveal that which is obscure—to illuminate, clarify, and perhaps ennoble. As Picasso himself stated, "The purpose of art is washing the dust of daily life off our souls."

The Eye on Art series is intended to assist readers in understanding the various roles of art in society. Each volume offers an in-depth exploration of a major artistic movement, medium, figure, or profession. All books in the series are beautifully illustrated with full-color photographs and diagrams. Riveting narrative, clear technical explanation, informative sidebars, fully documented quotes, a bibliography, and a thorough index all provide excellent starting points for research and discussion. With these features, the Eye on Art series is a useful introduction to the world of art—a world that can offer both insight and inspiration.

Introduction

Why Use a Computer?

For nearly a century animators have basically used the same technique to make characters move on a movie screen: In a long and tedious process, they create thousands of individual drawings, known as cels, each showing the character's body moving just a fraction of an inch. When these images are photographed individually, then run through a movie projector at a high rate of speed, the character is brought to life.

Some of Hollywood's most successful films, including *Snow White and the Seven Dwarfs*, *The Lion King*, and *The Little Mermaid*, have been produced through the traditional cel-animation process. But in 1995 the world of animation started changing when developments in software and computers enabled animators to produce the film *Toy Story*. It was the first movie completely animated on the computer. Now, virtually all feature-length animated films produced by Hollywood studios are accomplished through computer animation.

The work is still long and tedious. The production of a major Hollywood feature takes the skills of hundreds of artists, engineers, and technicians sometimes years to complete. Movies made by computer animation are expensive to produce. For example, the budget of the computer-animated film *Happy Feet*, which tells the story of a dancing penguin named Mumble, cost its studio some $100 million to produce before the film made its debut in 2006.

So why put all that money, effort, and talent into a genre of filmmaking that has survived for decades without the need for a keyboard and monitor? The answer is clear to anyone who has ever sat awestruck in a theater, watching the magic unfold on the screen: Computers have an enormous ability to expand the talent of the artist to show detail, movement, and color previously unavailable by human hand.

The most dramatic difference between computer animation and traditional cel animation is that an image generated by a computer can bring a three-dimensional quality to the film. In cel animation, the camera merely photographs a series of two-dimensional drawings layered over a painted, static background. In computer animation, the viewpoint of the background changes as the characters move through the scene. According to film critic Rick Lyman, "The result looks less like paint on paper than a film of a moving sculpture, existing in a real world of light and space."[1]

The computer-animated film *Happy Feet* cost its makers $100 million but it earned twice that amount at the box office.

Never Replace the Pencil

There are many ways in which the animator creates the three-dimensional world of the computer-animated film. The film *Happy Feet*, for example, was produced through a process known as motion capture. To animate the dancing penguins, the producers first filmed the motions and feet of world-class tap dancer Savion Glover. Then, the images of Glover were digitally transferred into the motions made on the computer screen by the penguin. Therefore, it is not really Mumble dancing on the screen, it is Glover—although the audience sees only the penguin. "*Happy Feet* is a technological marvel," exclaims film critic John Hayes. "Using a 'photo-reality' technique, in which real dancers are filmed and animation mimics their moves, the ice sheet becomes a giant disco."[2]

Happy Feet proved to be extremely successful, garnering some $200 million at the box office. In 2007 the film won the Academy Award for Best Animated Feature. Since the film achieved such a technological brilliance and earned so much money for its studio, it appears the future for traditional animation is dim. But that is not necessarily the case. Another film that won an Academy Award in 2007 was *The Danish Poet*, which received the Oscar for Best Animated Short Film. The fifteen-minute film was produced through the traditional method of animation, in which thousands of drawings were made by hand, although the filmmakers did use the computer to refine and color the images after they were produced. Still, in winning the award, *The Danish Poet*, which tells the story of a poet's quest for creativity, beat out several other contenders that were produced entirely through the computer-animation process. So it is still possible to produce high-quality and critically acclaimed animation by hand.

Even the Walt Disney Company realizes that traditional animation still has a future. The Disney studio, which for decades led all American studios in the production of cel-animated films, spent $7 billion in 2006 to acquire Pixar, the country's leading computer-animation studio. It would seem that Disney will now devote its entire resources to computer

animation, but in 2009 the studio expects to release *The Frog Princess*. The film will be produced the old-fashioned way, through cel art.

In fact, even computer animators know the importance of traditional artistic techniques to the digital-animation process. Most computer animators learned how to animate on the computer after they learned how to draw and paint. In most cases, computer animators know how to use the software to create and manipulate their animations, but they know very little about how that software was created. The development of software as well as the equipment for computer animation is a job better left to mathematicians, engineers, and others who possess a technical expertise that is usually far beyond the skills of most artists.

Therefore, art is still the primary skill needed by the computer animator. Says Roy Disney, a longtime Hollywood executive and the nephew of Disney studio founder Walt Disney, "The new world the computer has opened up to all of us is nothing more than the biggest, most diverse paint box yet available to artists. It has most certainly not—nor will it ever— replace the pencil."[3]

The Danish Poet is an example of traditional hand-drawn animation at its best.

1

The Computer Takes Over

When the film *Toy Story* was released in 1995, it marked the first time a full-length animated feature had been produced entirely by computer. There is no question that *Toy Story* presented a much different type of image to audiences. The computer gave the characters Woody and Buzz a three-dimensional perspective that moviegoers were not used to seeing in the traditional forms of animation.

Computer animation did not make its debut in *Toy Story*. In fact, engineers found ways to animate images by using computers as far back as the 1950s. At the time, the earliest developers of computer animation did not see the entertainment value in the craft. They believed computer animation would be put to much more practical uses, such as assisting designers of weapons and other military hardware. But by the 1970s commercial artists started employing the techniques of computer animation. Their work first started showing up in television commercials, mostly at the end of the spots, when a computer-generated image of the sponsor's logo appeared on the screen.

As computers and software became more sophisticated, and as artists and entertainment executives started seeing the potential of computer animation, what had started out as a tiny specialty in the animation industry soon came to dominate cinematic entertainment. In 2004, nine years after *Toy Story* was released, the computer-animated film *Shrek 2* earned $436 million at the box office, making it the most commercially successful animated movie in history. In fact, by 2007 eight of the ten top-grossing animated films of all time had been produced through computer animation.

Cel-Animation Pioneers

Prior to the development of computer animation, most animated features were produced by drawing images on cels, which are placed against a nonmoving background and are photographed with movie film. For years the cels were made out of cellulose, which is the substance that gives plants their structure. Today, however, cels are composed of a synthetic substance known as acetate.

Cel animation is an extremely lengthy process. Even for the briefest features, thousands of cel drawings must be employed. Most animators shoot one cel per frame of film and

Shrek 2 captured the hearts of movie viewers, as illustrated by its resounding success at the box office.

then film the cartoon at a speed of twenty-four frames per second. Therefore, a five-minute cartoon would require 7,200 cel drawings; for a ninety-minute full-length feature film, artists must produce nearly 130,000 cels.

Today cel animation is produced virtually the same way it was in 1908 when a French director, Émile Cohl, composed a very brief animation he titled *Fantasmagorie*, which featured the antics of a clown. Cohl produced the film using just seven hundred drawings. In 1911 American newspaper cartoonist Winsor McCay developed a two-minute animated film titled *Little Nemo*, which featured one of his comic-strip characters. McCay drew each image for each frame of film himself. McCay was the first animator to realize the enormous commercial potential of the medium. Soon after producing *Little Nemo*, he animated other features and took them on a tour of vaudeville theaters.

A page from Winsor McCay's comic strip *Little Nemo in Slumberland*. McCay did a short animated film based on the strip.

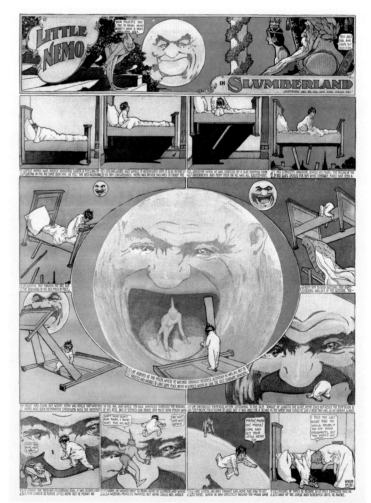

Of course, the animator given the most credit for developing the art form is Walt Disney, who produced the cartoon *Steamboat Willie* in 1928. The animated feature introduces the character Mickey Mouse as he navigates a rusty old boat over a choppy river. It was an immediate hit among audiences. Animation historian Charles Solomon says, "Disney managed to book it into the Colony Theatre in New York for two weeks. *Steamboat Willie* premiered on November 18, 1928, and the rest is animation history. The cartoon was a smash hit. Audiences were delighted with the bold little mouse who did a jaunty little clog step and played 'Turkey in the Straw' on a cow's teeth."[4] By today's standards, *Steamboat Willie* is regarded as fairly rudimentary animation. The film was produced in black and white. It employed many techniques that print cartoonists had been using for years. For example, when Mickey uses a barrel as a drum, striking it with a hammer, the artist illustrated the beat of the drum by showing dotted lines shooting out from the drum surface. As Solomon explains, "It is difficult to look at *Steamboat Willie* today and imagine how boldly innovative it must have appeared in 1928."[5]

Steamboat Willie established Disney's studio as the preeminent animator of its day, and the studio has maintained that status for decades by becoming one of the industry's top innovators. By the early 1930s animators had started employing simple colors in their features. The Disney studio produced the first multicolor cartoon, *Mickey's Band Concert*, in 1935, followed by the first feature-length animated film, *Snow White and the Seven Dwarfs*, in 1937.

The Whirlwind Project

Through the efforts of Disney and other creative people, cel animation became the standard for the industry. But other artists were also experimenting with alternative animation techniques. Starting in the early 1900s, many artists were drawn to the technique of stop-motion animation, which employs the use of puppets made out of clay or a similar malleable substance. The puppets are photographed moving through a scene. As with cel animation, twenty-four frames are shot per second. It means the animator must move each puppet at least twenty-four times to produce one second of film. If there are two or three puppets in the scene, and each puppet is using his or her mouth, hands, or feet, there could be tens of thousands of manipulations required to produce a film that runs a few minutes.

Stop-motion animation proved to be a highly sophisticated form of art. In the 1920s and 1930s, stop-motion animators were put to work by major Hollywood studios to produce images for some of the most popular horror movies of all time, including *King Kong* in 1933. In the film, pioneering animator Willis O'Brien used the stop-motion technique to create the giant ape Kong as well as the dinosaurs of Skull Island. The Kong puppet stood a mere 18 inches (45.7cm) tall, but O'Brien's skill transformed it into a larger-than-life beast that truly terrorized audiences of the era. Film critic Todd McCarthy states, "*Kong* was one of the sensations of its era, and Willis O'Brien's stop-motion special effects set a standard that went unsurpassed for decades."[6]

Following World War II, television exploded as an entertainment medium in the United States and elsewhere, and animators responded by providing programming for the new television networks. By the 1950s such animated cartoon shows as *Crusader Rabbit*, *The Heckle and Jeckle Show*, and *The Woody Woodpecker Show*, as well as the stop-motion show *Gumby*, had arrived on television. While children rushed home from school each day to watch the antics of their favorite cartoon characters, events were unfolding in large university computer laboratories that would eventually have a dramatic impact on the entertainment world.

Indeed, starting in the 1930s, at a time when audiences were awestruck by the animation of *Snow White and the Seven Dwarfs* or the stop-motion effects of *King Kong*, computers were first starting to come into use. One of the first computers, Harvard University's Mark I, was 50 feet (15.25m) long, weighed 5 tons (4,535kg), and took as long as twelve seconds

THE ECONOMICS OF ANIMATION

Computer animation is expensive. In 1995, the Pixar and Disney studios spent a combined $75 million to produce Toy Story. In comparison, Beauty and the Beast, which includes a few scenes animated by the computer but was mostly produced through cel art, cost some $30 million to produce.

But there can be a savings in computer animation that does not show up in the initial cost of production. In cel animation, once the film is finished the cels have no more use. In computer animation, all of the images are stored in the computer's memory. They can be resurrected at any time and used for other purposes. Toy Story, for example, spawned a sequel, Toy Story 2, as well as a planned third film slated for release in 2010. Also, the character of Buzz starred in his own sequel and in a television show. In addition, Toy Story was adapted into three electronic games, and many of the characters from the film were adapted into dolls and other toys.

For all of those uses, the images of Buzz, Woody, and the other characters could be extracted from the computer and used again. Journalists Brent Schlender and Jane Furth write:

Stored in the computer, they can be reproduced and adapted economically and infinitely, in film and video sequels and spinoff products like toys, TV shows, and CD-ROM games. Pixar's techniques so dramatically reduce the amount of manual labor required to make high-quality cartoons that they may well change the economics of animation.

Brent Schlender and Jane Furth, "Steve Jobs' Amazing Movie Adventure," *Fortune*, September 18, 1995, p. 154.

to compute the simplest mathematical problem. During World War II computer technology took a great leap forward with the development of the University of Pennsylvania's Electronic Numerical Integrator and Computer (ENIAC), which was able to perform one hundred thousand calculations a second. ENIAC weighed thirty tons (27,215kg) and required so much electricity that it occasionally dimmed the lights throughout Philadelphia. ENIAC was developed with the help of funding from the U.S. military, which hoped to use the computer's data to pinpoint targets for artillery gunners. The war ended before the computer was finished; nevertheless, the government liked what it had seen by then, and during the next few years most computer-science research projects would be funded by the military. Back in the 1950s, the notion that computers could one day develop animation for the entertainment industry was not likely to be on the minds of many people.

In 1951 a project at the Massachusetts Institute of Technology (MIT) known as Whirlwind produced a rudimentary flight simulator for the U.S. Navy. At the time, computers did not feature screens, but the MIT engineers were able to transfer

Computer technology took a great leap forward with the development of ENIAC (pictured) during World War II.

the data to the screen of an oscilloscope, which could display simple graphics. Oscilloscopes had been used for many years to display impulses of electrical current produced by industrial equipment and similar devices.

The image on the Whirlwind screen depicted the eastern coast of Massachusetts while a symbol "flying" over the coast was a simulated aircraft. A major development in the project was the light pen. When the light pen was pointed at the simulated aircraft, Whirlwind produced text on the screen that identified the plane as well as its speed and direction.

Hummingbird Takes Flight

Scientists working at other university laboratories developed similar projects. In 1956 scientists at the University of Michigan were able to simulate the movements of military vehicles. In 1958 MIT scientists working under a U.S. Air Force contract developed a technique to print out computer-generated pictures. Meanwhile, corporations started exploring computer imaging as well. In 1959 engineers at General Motors produced computer-generated drawings that were displayed on ordinary 35mm film. A year later a scientist at Boeing Aircraft, William Fetter, coined the term "computer graphics"[7] to describe the work he had been doing in designing the cockpits of airplanes.

By this time, computers were starting to employ screens to display text as well as graphics. In 1960 the Digital Equipment Company, one of the first computer manufacturers in the world, introduced the first computer equipped with a monitor—the Program Data Processor-1. It sold for $120,000. The Digital Equipment Company also equipped the device with a keyboard.

Meanwhile, other innovators developed techniques that would prove to be important to computerized filmmaking. In 1960 filmmaker John Whitney Sr. adapted a computer-driven device that aimed an antiaircraft gun for use with a camera; using high-contrast photographic film, Whitney was able to produce abstract art.

In 1964 Ohio State University art professor Charles Csuri found himself awestruck by an image printed in a publication produced by the school's electrical engineering department. The image showed the profile of a female face. It had been produced on a rudimentary printer that resembled a typewriter. By using just a few letters of the alphabet, the programmer was able to fabricate the image and color it in shades of gray. "When I saw that first picture," recalls Csuri, "I could not believe what I was looking at. I saw the implications, and it hit me like a bolt of lightning. I immediately enrolled in a computer programming course."[8]

In those days, before the widespread use of keyboards, most data were entered into a computer through punch cards, which consisted of small cardboard cards with holes placed in various points. The holes in the cards were read by the computer, which produced information based on what the punch cards instructed it to do. Once he learned the basics of programming, Csuri generated printouts of drawings by inputting tens of thousands of punch cards into the Ohio State computer. In fact, Csuri was able to instruct the computer to simulate paintings by such renowned artists as Pablo Picasso, Paul Klee, and Francisco Goya.

In 1967 Csuri programmed the computer to produce a short animated film titled *Hummingbird*. The computer generated thirty thousand images, which were then transferred right to movie film. The movie, which showed a rendering of a hummingbird in flight, was the first true computer-generated animation. A year after Csuri produced the film, it was obtained by the Museum of Modern Art in New York, where it has remained a part of the museum's permanent collection.

Pixilated Images

Anybody who saw *Hummingbird* may have laughed at the notion that computers could ever replace animation produced by the human hand. The art in Csuri's film is crude: *Hummingbird* was rendered entirely in white line drawings on a black background. The film is also brief, lasting just ten min-

CHARLES CSURI

Ohio State University art professor Charles Csuri launched the era of computer animation in 1967 when he produced a ten-minute film depicting a hummingbird in flight. Born in 1922, Csuri loved to draw but never expected to become an artist. He grew up the son of a shoemaker in Cleveland, Ohio, and was able to attend college at Ohio State because he received a football scholarship.

His college career was interrupted by World War II. He was awarded a Bronze Star for heroism during the Battle of the Bulge, which was the last major German offensive of the war. Returning to Ohio State after the war, Csuri completed his education and joined the faculty, where he shared an office with Roy Lichtenstein, who would go on to be a major figure in American abstract art.

After producing *Hummingbird*, Csuri continued to experiment with computer graphics. In the twenty-five years following production of the film, the National Science Foundation awarded Csuri several grants totaling $25 million to continue the development of computer animation. Many of his students have gone on to careers in computer graphics, including Jeff Light, who created the dinosaurs for the film *Jurassic Park* as well as the ghosts in the movie *Casper.*

Charles Csuri's short film of hummingbird flight launched the era of computer animation.

utes, and there is no story—it simply shows the motions of the bird in flight. As Csuri screened *Hummingbird* for audiences on the Ohio State campus, Disney's hit animated movie *The Jungle Book* debuted in theaters, and on television, the popular Marvel Comics superhero *Spider-Man* was animated into a Saturday morning show. Indeed, the cel animation for *The Jungle Book* provided vibrant colors and plenty of action. The film also included the voices of big-name stars, hit songs, and a plot the audience could follow. On television, the cel-animated *Spider-Man* proved to be a hit and was renewed by the ABC television network for two more seasons.

But there was interest in the entertainment community to push computer animation into new and creative directions. At first, most of the interest was generated by the producers of television commercials. Typically, television commercials conclude with an image of the sponsor's corporate logo, and these were the first computer-generated images that started appearing in commercials during the 1970s. An example occurred in 1974, when the Levi's sportswear company produced a television commercial featuring an actor, dressed in Levi's blue jeans, walking the Levi's logo on a leash. The movements of the actor were filmed, but a computer generated the image of the logo, which was merged into the film.

Elsewhere in the entertainment industry, great strides were being made in using the computer to enhance special effects on film. At first, filmmakers did not concentrate on animated movies, but the techniques they learned by producing computer-generated imagery (CGI) would soon be applied to animated features.

The first film to employ CGI was *Westworld*, which was released in 1973. *Westworld* tells the story of a futuristic amusement park where guests can play the parts of Wild West characters. In the amusement park, some of the characters are portrayed by robots. *Westworld* features scenes from the robots' points of view. To show the audience what the robot is seeing, the camera image was scrambled by the computer, showing pixilated images. In 1977 a much more ambitious film featuring CGI was released by a Hollywood studio. The title of the film was *Star Wars*.

Destroying the *Death Star*

The film made cinematic history. The story of intergalactic rebels fighting against an evil empire generated a worldwide audience that was suddenly hungry for science-fiction adventures. It also set a very high benchmark for CGI, featuring sophisticated scenes of animation that were produced by the computer.

By now, the hardware and software needed to produce computer animation had developed far beyond the machinery and techniques that Csuri had used to produce *Hummingbird* just a decade before. By no means was *Star Wars* an animated film, however; it featured actors, life-size props and sets, and live-action filming. The director, George Lucas, made wide use of miniatures and other well-established special-effects techniques. But Lucas did merge several computer-animated scenes into the final print of the film. For example, in the closing minutes of the film the hero, Luke Skywalker, must navigate a jet fighter over the mechanical terrain of the *Death Star*

Luke Skywalker's jet fighter flies over the *Death Star* in this computer-generated image from *Star Wars*.

on his way to dropping a torpedo into an exhaust port of the ship. The surface of the *Death Star* was generated by a computer; in the film, the terrain speeds by under Skywalker's jet fighter as the hero evades enemy fighters. It took the computer animators a month to produce two minutes of footage; just forty seconds were used in the final cut of the film. And the last four seconds of the sequence—the moment when the torpedo falls into the core of the *Death Star*—were drawn by hand. Still, there is no question that *Star Wars* revolutionized the use of CGI. Film critic Charles Champlin says, "It was the extraordinary abundance of visual and aural special effects that lifted the film past anything that had been done before."[9]

As audiences stood in long lines to see *Star Wars*, the animation industry in America had become somewhat tired and stagnant. The industry leader, Disney, had released a number of films that received lukewarm praise from critics as well as cool receptions from audiences. After the success of *The Jungle Book*—which over the years has earned Disney more than $200 million—the studio produced *Robin Hood* in 1973 and *The Many Adventures of Winnie the Pooh* in 1977. *Robin Hood* included scenes from an earlier aborted Disney film titled *Reynard the Fox*. Likewise, *The Many Adventures of Winnie the Pooh* was actually a feature-length film spliced together from scenes drawn from three shorter Disney cartoons starring the characters created by author A.A. Milne.

There was no shortage of dissent at the Disney studio. In 1979 leading animator Don Bluth, believing Disney had lost its creative edge, quit the studio and formed his own production company to compete against Disney. He would soon produce such cel-animated films as *The Secret of N.I.M.H.* and *An American Tail.*

The Arrival of Pixar

Not only did there seem to be a dearth of creativity in animated films, but there was a dearth of technological advances as well. By the end of the 1970s there had been some advancements in cel animation, most notably through the process of photographing a number of cels in the same frame of film, which gave the images much more detail. Nevertheless, animated movies were still basically produced by teams of artists inking images onto thousands of acetate cels.

As Lucas worked on his sequel to *Star Wars*, titled *The Empire Strikes Back*, he established his own special-effects company to develop the CGI for his films as well as other studios willing to hire his services. He named the company Industrial Light and Magic. In 1979 Lucas created a division of Industrial Light and Magic to concentrate solely on developing techniques and equipment that filmmakers could use to produce CGI effects. The division, which he called the Graphics Group, developed some truly advanced research. Nonetheless, in 1986 Lucas decided to sell the division because it was losing money. Lucas opted to concentrate more on making movies and less on developing research for other moviemakers.

He sold the Graphics Group for $5 million to Steve Jobs, one of the founders of Apple Computers. Jobs invested another $5 million of his own money and renamed the company Pixar. Jobs was initially interested in developing hardware that could produce animated images, which he believed would have use in the defense and medical industries. But one of the company's earliest customers turned out to be the Disney studio, which employed Pixar's hardware as well as software of its own development to produce images for its animated films. Disney was the first studio to use a computer to produce the images that its cel artists had been doing for years. That does not mean Disney stopped using cel artists altogether, but it was clear that computers were starting to change the industry. In 1984 Disney produced *The Little Mermaid* mostly through the "ink and paint" process; but the final shot of the film, which depicts the wedding scene of Prince Eric and Ariel, was produced through a computer.

Pixar's hardware never sold well, but executives of the company saw the enormous potential of what Disney was starting to do. Pixar developed its own software and became an independent

Computer animation added three-dimensional perspective to this scene from *Beauty and the Beast.*

film production company, first making computer animation for television commercials and then expanding into feature films. In 1991 the Disney studio's film *Beauty and the Beast* included sequences produced by Pixar's computers. Most of the film was produced through the cel-animation method, but the backgrounds in the ballroom sequence—in which Belle first dances with the Beast—were rendered by computer animation. If the ballroom scene had been hand-painted by artists, it would have been a flat, two-dimensional rendering. The characters would simply have danced across a static background. By using a computer, the filmmakers were able to add a three-dimensional perspective to the background, changing the viewpoint of the scenery as the two characters danced through it. As *Beauty and the Beast* producer Don Hahn relates:

The ballroom sequence is the bonding moment of the film when the two main characters finally get together. For us filmmakers, the computer offered us a way to get heightened emotions on the screen and more dramatic effects than we could have gotten conventionally. It allowed us to move the camera around and take a look at the room instead of just looking at a flat piece of artwork. Technology as a whole is an extension of our fingers, hands and minds. Computer graphics let us go beyond what we can currently achieve with pencil and paper or paint and a brush.[10]

The dazzling computer animation included in the film helped *Beauty and the Beast* earn an Academy Award nomination for Best Picture in 1992—making it the first animated film ever to receive an Oscar nomination in that category.

A year later the Disney film *Aladdin* made even more use of computer animation. In the film, Pixar computers provided the animated sequences inside the genie's cave and also produced every image of the magic carpet that is featured in the film. It was the first time a complete character in a feature film was animated by the computer.

Buzz and Woody

After the success of *Beauty and the Beast* and *Aladdin*, it became clear to executives at Pixar and Disney that a full-length feature film could be produced entirely on the computer. In 1995 Pixar and Disney partnered to produce *Toy Story*. The story features the adventures of toys that come to life when the little boy who owns them is not in the room. The film features the voices of Tom Hanks as Woody, the toy cowboy, and Tim Allen as Buzz Lightyear, the toy space ranger.

After Hanks and Allen read the dialogue in a recording studio, some three hundred technicians spent a total of eight hundred thousand hours behind their computer screens, fashioning the artwork for the eighty-one-minute movie. Indeed, it took up to fifteen hours of work to produce each frame of film. There is no question, though, that in *Toy Story*, audiences saw a breed of animation unfold on the screen that they had never seen before. Film critic Roger Ebert explains:

> Imagine the spectacular animation of the ballroom sequence in *Beauty and Beast* at feature length and you'll get the idea. The movie doesn't simply animate

Toy Story represented a new level of computer animation, with fully animated characters and movements.

characters in front of painted backdrops: it fully animates the characters and the space they occupy, and allows its point of view to move freely around them. Computer animation has grown so skillful that sometimes you don't even notice it. . . . Here, you do notice it, because you're careening through space with a new sense of freedom.

Consider for example a scene where Buzz Lightyear, the new space toy, jumps off a bed, bounces off a ball, careens off a ceiling, spins around on a hanging toy helicopter and zooms into a series of loop-the-loops on a model car race track. Watch Buzz, the background, and the perspective—which stretches and contracts to manipulate the sense of speed. It's an amazing ride.[11]

In 2006 Disney agreed to buy Pixar for more than $7 billion—showing how important the computer-animation studio had become in the industry in the twenty years since Lucas agreed to sell the company to Jobs for $5 million. Today Pixar faces competition from more than a dozen computer-animation companies, some of which are underwritten by Hollywood's most important studios. One of Pixar's main competitors is the computer-animation division of DreamWorks, the studio founded by director Steven Spielberg, which has produced *Shrek* and *Shrek 2*, which together have earned more than $700 million at the box office. Today such computer-animated films as *Cars*, *Finding Nemo*, *Happy Feet*, *Monsters, Inc.*, and *The Incredibles* are among the highest-grossing animated films in the history of American cinema. They are all products of an industry that was launched just some forty years ago during the ten-minute flight of a hummingbird.

2

Games: Computer Animation Comes Home

A wide receiver streaks down the sideline, dodging tacklers as he eyes the goal line. A squad of commandos steps carefully through war-torn streets, evading sniper fire as it roots out terrorists. A plumber named Super Mario outsmarts an evil prehistoric turtle named King Koopa. Wearing pistols on her hips, long-legged Lara Croft battles evil spirits, assorted mythological creatures, and lifelike gangsters.

Players of electronic games are quite familiar with those scenarios and characters. Indeed, electronic games have come a long way since the days when players dropped quarters in a machine so they could spend countless hours playing *Pong*. And yet *Pong*—a virtual version of Ping Pong that tested little more than a player's hand-eye coordination—is as much a product of computer animation as Super Mario and Lara Croft.

Of course, what makes computer games different from the animation that is seen on the movie screen is their interactive component. Sitting at home, players can direct the scenarios and action. Still, the techniques and equipment used to produce games are similar to the techniques employed by animators to create films and television shows. Recent advancements in technology have enabled artists to provide highly sophisticated animation for electronic games that have helped interactive entertainment become a $13-billion-a-year industry. Science journalist Keith Ferrell states, "Graphics, sound, motion: All must come together to create a believable illusion. The goal, some feel, is interactive fiction as striking in image and sound as motion pictures."[12]

The Birth of Atari

Interactive electronic games actually date back to 1947, when engineers Thomas T. Goldsmith Jr. and Estle Ray Mann figured out a way to control a point of light that traveled across the screen of an early television set. Goldsmith and Mann worked for DuMont Laboratories, an early manufacturer of television sets. They developed a process to control the path of the light by adjusting knobs on the front of the screen. In this earliest of games, the light represented a missile. Since the game players had no means to create graphics on the screen, the "targets" were provided in a clear plastic overlay that was placed atop the screen. Still, players could aim missiles at targets, although the scorekeeping had to be accomplished with pencil and paper. Goldsmith and Mann patented the game, which they called the Cathode-Ray Tube Amusement Device. (A cathode-ray tube was the device inside early televisions that brought the picture to life on the screen.) DuMont went out of business in 1960, long before the company had a chance to enter the electronic games market.

In 1961 a group of students at the Massachusetts Institute of Technology used the school's new Program Data Processor-1 (PDP-1) computer to develop a game they called *Spacewar!* The game featured the simplest of graphics—basically points of light on the screen—but players could maneuver a spaceship around a star while battling enemy ships. The PDP-1's manufacturer, the Digital Equipment Company, eventually received permission from the students to distribute the game along with the PDP-1. Therefore, anybody who had access to a PDP-1 could play *Spacewar!* Of course, since a PDP-1 computer cost $120,000, the game was played mostly in university

Born in 1943, Nolan Bushnell became one of the founders of the electronic game industry when he developed *Pong* and established Atari. He got hooked on games as a college student, playing *Spacewar!* on the computers at the University of Utah, where he received an engineering degree in 1968. Describing the development of *Pong*, Bushnell says, "I made it with my own two hands and a soldering iron."

Bushnell started Atari with a partner, Ted Dabney. Each man contributed $250. In 1976 Bushnell sold Atari to Warner Communications for $28 million.

Although Atari provided Bushnell with a financial windfall, he did make one very bad business decision while running the company. Most of the earliest employees of Atari were young men and women who were eager to get in on the ground floor of the booming computer industry. One of Bushnell's first employees was Steve Jobs, who dropped out of college in his freshman year to join the company. Later, Jobs and a friend, Steve Wozniak, built a simple home computer, calling it the Apple 1. They asked Bushnell if he would invest in their idea, but Bushnell declined. Jobs and Wozniak would go on to establish Apple as one of the world's largest manufacturers of computers and other electronic equipment, including the iPod.

Nolan Bushnell, shown here with an Androbot, helped create the electronic game industry.

Quoted in David Sheff, *Game Over: How Nintendo Zapped an American Industry, Captured Your Dollars, and Enslaved Your Children.* New York: Random House, 1993, p. 135.

laboratories, corporate computer departments, military installations, and other institutions that could afford expensive computer equipment. As such, it was not available in the consumer market. Still, during the 1960s engineers and software designers continued to experiment with manipulating images on computer screens, knowing that eventually electronic games could be fashioned for home players.

One *Spacewar!* fan was University of Utah engineering student Nolan Bushnell.

After graduating in 1968, Bushnell and a friend, Ted Dabney, adapted *Spacewar!* to play on an ordinary black-and-white television set and renamed it *Computer Space*. They developed a hardware console that hooked to the television. The console—a rudimentary computer—could do nothing more than play the game on the television. They formed a company named Syzygy to sell the game, but they were able to sell just a few models. Players found the instructions too difficult, and Syzygy was soon out of business.

Bushnell and Dabney learned a valuable lesson from the failure of *Computer Space,* and they resolved to develop a new game that would be more user-friendly. Bushnell recalls, "To be successful, I had to come up with a game people already knew how to play."[13] They each contributed $250 and started a new company, which they named Atari—the word for a maneuver in the Japanese board game Igo—and the first game they developed was an electronic version of Ping-Pong, which they called *Pong*.

Instead of building new consoles for home sales, Bushnell and Dabney released *Pong* as an arcade game. They envisioned it standing next to pinball machines in taverns, soda shops, and bowling alleys. A *Pong* machine was nothing more than a blank screen that featured a white dot smacked back and forth by the players, who used knobs to control the two virtual paddles. There were even sound effects; when a player hit the "ball," the machine emitted a definitive "plink."

In 1972 the first *Pong* game was installed in a bar named Andy Capp's in San Jose, California. Bushnell and Dabney set up the *Pong* console next to a pinball machine. There was one line of instruction printed alongside the screen: "Avoid missing ball for high score."[14] Minutes after the installers turned the game on, two bar patrons wandered over, studied the curious machine, and dropped in the first quarter. It took the players a few quarters to get used to the controls, but within minutes they were playing a vigorous game of virtual Ping-Pong. When the two players finally exhausted their supply of quarters, they discovered a long line of bar patrons had formed behind them.

By the second day, the machine had broken from overuse. Bushnell and Dabney returned to fix it. They also installed a larger coin box. At the end of the first week, the *Pong* machine earned the two inventors three hundred dollars. The pinball machine standing nearby took in a mere thirty dollars during the same period. Word soon spread throughout San Jose, and within days the bar was jammed with young adults eager to drop quarters into the *Pong* machine's slot. Eventually Atari manufactured some nineteen thousand *Pong* machines and sold them mostly to bowling alleys and bars.

Super Mario

Developments occurred quickly. Atari grew into a major manufacturer of arcade games and soon entered the home-consumer market as well. The company developed a home version of *Pong* in 1975; it connected to a television set through a component that could easily be attached to the terminals for the television antenna. Two years later Atari manufactured a home console, the Atari 2600, that accepted game cartridges. It was a tremendous step forward in game technology. Now a console did not have to be dedicated to a single game but could play a wide variety of games. Players controlled the action with a joystick, which took its name from the main steering device found in airplane cockpits. Using the joystick, players could start and stop the action, change the direction of their characters, and, if the game required it, fire a weapon by pushing a button on the stick or its base.

Among the games available for the Atari 2600 were *Pac-Man*, which called on players to send a hungry, round-headed

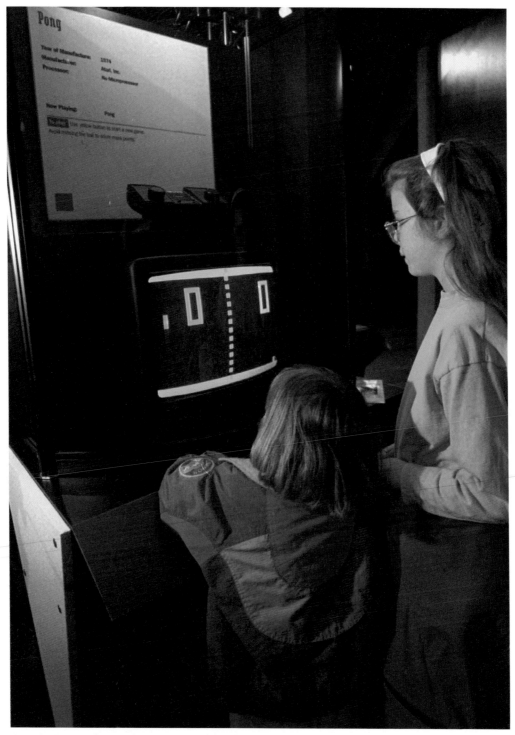

Atari's *Pong*, shown here, was an instant hit.

character through a maze while he gobbled up points; *Space Invaders*, in which players fired missiles at descending lines of alien attackers; and *Breakout*, an advancement on *Pong* that required players to make bricks in a wall disappear by ricocheting a ball against them with a paddle. In the first year the Atari 2600 was on the market, the company sold some 250,000 of the machines at a price of about two hundred dollars each; by 1979 Atari was selling a million consoles a year.

Some of the early games for the Atari 2600 and its competitors were designed by Japanese artists and engineers who were part of a booming home-electronics industry in that country. One of those companies was Nintendo, which had been founded in the 1880s as a manufacturer of playing cards. Over the years Nintendo's owners steered the company into a number of different businesses—including managing hotels and taxicabs and selling rice—before finding its niche as a toy maker. In 1975 Nintendo obtained the rights to sell an American-made game console, the Magnavox Odyssey, in Japan.

The graphics produced by the Atari 2600, the Magnavox Odyssey, and the other early systems were miles ahead of the dots of white light found in *Spacewar!* and even *Pong*. By today's standards, they were still rather simple. *Pac-Man* was, after all, little more than a yellow ball with a continually chomping mouth. Still, there was a definite art component to designing the games. In Japan, executives at Nintendo negotiated with King Features, the owner of the animated cartoons and comic books featuring Popeye, to convert the spinach-munching sailor into an electronic game character. When the negotiations fell through, Nintendo decided to develop a game featuring a character of its own design. In 1977 the company handed the job to its lone staff artist, twenty-four-year-old Sigeru Miyamoto.

Miyamoto was delighted to tackle the assignment. As an art student at the Kanazawa College of Industrial Arts and Crafts, he had poured many coins into the arcade games near campus. Miyamoto loved playing arcade games and believed he could improve on the graphics found in *Space Invaders* and *Pac-Man*.

Sigeru Miyamoto grew up in the small town of Sonebe in Japan. Miyamoto's family was of modest means; they did not own a car or a television set. For entertainment, the Miyamotos would take a train to the city of Kyoto every few months to see movies. As a boy, Miyamoto recalled seeing *Peter Pan* and *Snow White and the Seven Dwarfs*.

Born in 1952, the artist who would later design *Donkey Kong* and other hit games for Nintendo aspired to be either a painter or a puppeteer. He carried pencils and sketch pads with him constantly and would often wander alone in parks and other scenic places near his home, finding a place where he could sit and sketch for hours.

In 1977, after Miyamoto graduated from college, his father contacted an old friend, Hiroshi Yamauchi, who ran Nintendo. Yamauchi agreed to interview Miyamoto, and he was impressed with the young man's talent. He hired Miyamoto, but he made little use of the artist's abilities until 1980, when he asked him to design the characters for a new video game. Miyamoto came up with Super Mario, Princess Pauline, and Donkey Kong, the barrel-rolling gorilla. Following the creation of *Donkey Kong*, Miyamoto remained with Nintendo and has been instrumental in designing many of the company's top games, including *Legend of Zelda*.

Nintendo game designer Sigeru Miyamoto plays Legend of Zelda, *a game he designed.*

As a young boy, one of Miyamoto's favorite stories was "Beauty and the Beast." He let his mind wander and concocted a villain in the form of a beast—a big, goofy ape. The object of the game, he decided, would be for the player to rescue a princess from the ape. To save the princess, the player would have to leap over barrels and other obstacles that the ape tossed in the way. Each time the hero jumped over a barrel, he would score a point for the player.

Next, Miyamoto worked on the design of the main character—the hero whose movements would be controlled by the player. Working with the engineers at Nintendo, Miyamoto knew that their ability to adapt graphics to the game screen was still quite limited. So to stand out against the background of the scene, the character would have to include oversized features. The engineers also warned Miyamoto against drawing long or bouncy hairstyles—they were difficult to animate. He filled many notebooks with sketches and finally drew a short, stout fellow with a large nose and floppy moustache. Instead of hair, Miyamoto drew the character wearing a bright red hat.

To name the game, Miyamoto proposed to use the word *Kong* in the title because it suggested the image of an ape. He also flipped through a Japanese-English dictionary and found the word *donkey*, which in Japanese means "stupid" or "goofy." And so he had the name for the game: *Donkey Kong*.

Nintendo elected to produce *Donkey Kong* as an arcade game. It took four years for *Donkey Kong* to progress from Miyamoto's sketches to the assembly line, where the game was installed in arcade consoles and then shipped to America. Upon arriving in the United States, two thousand of the *Donkey Kong* consoles were stored in a warehouse in Seattle, Washington, while an American Nintendo marketing team worked out the details for selling the units. Part of their job was to develop an English text of instructions for American players. They decided to give the characters in the game English names. The ape could still be named Donkey Kong. The princess would be Pauline, named after the wife of a Nintendo employee in the United States. But when it came to naming the game's hero, they were stumped. Sitting around a card table in the Seattle warehouse, the American and Japanese Nintendo employees debated a number of different names. Suddenly, there was a knock on the door. It was the owner of the warehouse, Mario Segali, who demanded the rent. Segali was quite angry and did not leave until he received assurances that his money would be forthcoming. As soon as the warehouse owner left, the Nintendo employees knew they had found the name for the game's hero: Super Mario.

Three-Dimensional Graphics

Donkey Kong proved to be enormously successful. The first two thousand arcade machines sold quickly; another sixty thousand were soon shipped from Japan. In the first two years, *Donkey Kong* earned Nintendo sales of more than $100 million. Soon after the game arrived in the United States, Nintendo licensed the title to Coleco, an American company, to produce a home version.

In fact, many of the most popular games were being produced for home consoles as well as personal computers, which were becoming more of a presence in American homes. Nintendo and the other game manufacturers found they could license the games to software companies, which adapted the

Filmmakers made more use of CGI in *The Empire Strikes Back* (pictured) than in the original *Star Wars* movie.

titles so they could be played on home computers. Now, a player could insert a floppy disk into his or her computer and play *Space Invaders* at home, using buttons on the keyboard to control the action on the screen.

By this time, CGI had become a big part of Hollywood moviemaking. The sequel to *Star Wars*, *The Empire Strikes Back*, featured far more CGI shots than the original. In the film audiences were dazzled by the backgrounds surrounding the Cloud City, which were created through computer animation. The filmmakers also used computers to animate the lightsabers wielded by the Jedi knights. And then, in 1983, the third film in the series, *Return of the Jedi*, included even more CGI effects—some seven hundred images that made it into the final film were produced on the computer. For example, late in the film, Luke and Leia race against Imperial Stormtroopers on gravity-defying jet bikes that zoom through a heavily wooded forest. In reality, most of the action for the scene was generated by animators working in front of computer screens. Film critic Charles Champlin says, "Probably most unforgettably, there were the Speeder Bikes whizzing through the forest a few feet off the ground representing a teenager's wildest dreams of excitement. The trickery worked so well that it is still hard to imagine that the Speeder Bike doesn't really exist and has simply not yet reached the consumer market."[15]

George Lucas, the producer of the *Star Wars* movies, realized that the characters and scenarios from the films could be adapted into games. He established LucasArts, a division of his entertainment company devoted to producing games. Such games as *X-Wing*, *Rebel Assault,* and *Dark Forces* were adapted from *Star Wars* scenarios. Lucas also produced the films in the Indiana Jones series. Two games featuring the swashbuckling archaeologist Indiana Jones were developed. By the 1990s game designers were able to provide far more graphics, speed, color, and action because of the advancements in computer technology—particularly the microprocessor, the tiny device in the computer that relays the user's commands to the computer, instructing the machine on what to do. Indeed, by the

1990s home computers had become very sophisticated and able to accept a high degree of graphics and animation. In 1996 hardware manufacturers added a microprocessor to home machines that enabled the monitors to display graphics in three dimensions. Now players could control animated characters—seeing them from all sides, and changing their viewpoints, directions, and paths through the games. After years of forcing Super Mario to dodge Donkey Kong's barrels, Nintendo designed other games featuring the character. In 1985 the company paired Mario with his brother, Luigi, and sent them off to battle a prehistoric turtle named King Koopa in a game titled *Super Mario Brothers*. With the improvement in computer graphics that arrived in the mid-1990s, players could spend hours directing Mario and Luigi through a complicated three-dimensional maze in search of King Koopa.

Tomb Raider

With the rise in popularity of the games, the characters started taking on lives of their own. In the beginning, game designers sought permission to adapt characters from other mediums into games. Now characters from games were being cast in movies and television shows. Mario and Luigi starred in a film version of their exploits in 1993. The game *Mortal Kombat* was adapted into a film in 1995. During the 1990s characters from the *Pokémon* and *Sonic the Hedgehog* games were adapted into children's animated television series. In 2001 *Tomb Raider's* plucky heroine, Lara Croft, was featured in a major Hollywood version of the game.

Tomb Raider made its debut as a game in November 1996, selling some 500,000 copies in its first two months on store shelves. Since then, updated *Tomb Raider* versions and its sequels have continued to dominate game sales. In 2006 the sequel *Tomb Raider Legend* sold nearly 3 million copies in the first five weeks of its release.

Lara Croft's designer was British artist Toby Gard. Originally, the firm designing the game, Core Design of Derby, England, proposed to feature a male character as the hero, but

The artist who designed the character of Lara Croft (pictured) wanted a strong, intelligent, crafty female protagonist.

Gard had been toying with the idea of a strong, intelligent, and crafty female protagonist. After working up some sketches of Lara, Gard sold Core Design on featuring a female protagonist for the game.

"My original design was a guy in some tombs," said Gard,

> but when I started doing proper designs the female character just worked better. . . . She was real different from the game characters of the time. Compared to the burly men shooting guns she had a real appeal. She was dangerous and had a danger about her that gave her a real difference to other female characters that were basically sex objects. Lara had a mystery about her. Also, I was very keen to get Lara to animate properly, which no one else at the time was doing. This made her move slowly but look realistic which helped players empathize with her.[16]

In fact, in working with Core Design's software engineers, Gard had to continually change the design of the character so she could be animated. For example, in the original design Lara's hair was braided, but the engineers convinced Gard to drop the braids because they would be too difficult to animate and would therefore require the consoles to work harder, which would slow down the action of the game. (In later versions of *Tomb Raider* and its sequels, Lara's hair is braided.) On the other hand, Gard wanted Lara's movements to be lifelike, so he studied how people walk, run, jump, and move their arms. Another innovation Gard brought to the game was to diverge from the practice of some action-packed games, like *Doom* and *Duke Nukem*, where the player views the scene from the main character's eyes. In *Tomb Raider*, Gard gave the player the viewpoint of looking over Lara's shoulder. Says Core Design artist Stuart Atkinson, "Toby did a fantastic job, not only because it's so realistic, but because he had to deal with a lot of technical challenges as well."[17]

Thanks to the popularity of the game as well as the film version starring Angelina Jolie as Lara Croft, the character has become something of a folk hero. Core Design engineer Adrian Smith relates, "We know from the success of *Tomb Raider* that the combination of different elements—exploration, puzzles and combat—works really well as it stands. The interaction is between the player and Lara; it's a very personal experience."[18]

The Insights of the Artist

Tomb Raider and other games are available in software versions that can be played on home computers. Games can also be played on the Internet. But to play the most sophisticated games, players know they need the dedicated consoles manufactured by such industry leaders as Nintendo, Sega, Sony, and Microsoft. Added to the action are the voices of actors whose lines are spoken throughout the game. Behind it all, though, are the animators, who use their skills to create the backgrounds and characters whose fates are controlled by the players. As for the games, most of them cover the genres of science fiction, sports, fantasy, adventure, and crime stories. The games

Nintendo game designer Sigeru Miyamoto once aspired to be a painter or puppeteer.

can be violent and are overwhelmingly aimed at male audiences, but in recent years game-production companies have started designing games for female players.

For example, in late 2006 an interactive version of the hit television show *Desperate Housewives* was released by game designer Buena Vista Games. The game features all the familiar back-stabbing housewives from the show. The player assumes the role of a new female neighbor on Wisteria Lane and must maneuver among her scheming neighbors to solve a mystery. In the game, the animators have depicted likenesses of the key actresses from the show.

The computer graphics produced by today's game designers are light years ahead of *Pong* and *Pac-Man*. Game players today—who can enhance their experiences by hooking their consoles to high-definition television sets—can maneuver their characters through some truly awe-inspiring, colorful graphics that depict distant planets, mystical underworlds, and dark, urban jungles. Since 1998 the Academy of Interactive Arts and Sciences has presented awards for outstanding achievement in game design. One of the awards is presented for outstanding achievement in animation. The 2007 winner of the animation award was *Gears of War*, which follows an elite squad of commandos and their leader, Marcus Fenix, who must save humans from alien killers on a distant planet. The game was manufactured to be played on Microsoft's Xbox 360 console. Yahoo game critic Mike Smith says *Gears of War* packs a lot of nonstop action, requiring players to be constantly firing and reloading their weapons:

Gears of War, winner of an outstanding achievement in animation award, boasts gorgeous visuals.

> Even reloading, usually a straightforward and functional process, comes in for a little extra love. Hitting the reload button triggers a little animation on the weapon's ammo gauge. Stop the bar in just the right

point, and the shells you're inserting get a useful damage bonus. . . .

Get too distracted by these interface details, though, and you'll miss *Gears of War*'s gorgeous visuals. From the bulging veins on Marcus's neck to the heat haze rising off his gun, superb isn't the word—it's easily the best looking 360 game to date, and doesn't seem to stress the hardware noticeably. If, like us, you've been drooling over the screen shots for months, be reassured: it really does look that good.[19]

As computer technology improves, experts believe the graphics produced for games will improve as well: Colors will become more vivid, the characters will become more lifelike, the action will move faster, and the images will become ever crisper. According to science journalist Keith Ferrell:

What we're looking for is a new art form, one that learns from the past while inventing its own future. Motion pictures, still in their first century, have become the dominant art form of our age. Perhaps interactive art can go as far. Perhaps, coupling the rapidly increasing power of the computer with the insights and abilities of the artist, it can go farther.[20]

Is It Art or Science?

3

When animators working on the film *Monsters, Inc.* designed the big blue character named Sully, they found it necessary to employ a unique computer program that enabled them to move each strand of Sully's fur—all 2.3 million of them. Writing the program involved the talents of dozens of software engineers and programmers, but in the end the animators were able to manipulate Sully's fur on their screens, making it curl on command.

This raises a key question: Is computer animation art or science? The answer is both, but they rarely mingle. For the most part, when it comes to computer animation the artists have their roles and the software engineers have theirs, and there is not much overlap.

Most animators working professionally today are graduates of art schools rather than computer science programs. Meanwhile, all software derives from mathematical formulas known as algorithms. Generally speaking, art schools do not spend a lot of their resources training students in algorithmic science. Since the earliest days of cel animation, animators have been artists. Although today the animation is produced on a computer, it is still a form of art.

The major animation studios have never lost sight of the fact that art provides the backbone of animation. At Pixar, the creator of *Monsters, Inc.*, executive vice president John Lasseter, says his company has invested heavily in technology, but the artists are the ones who provide Pixar with its cinematic vision. As Lasseter explains, "Here, the art challenges the technology and the technology inspires the art."[21]

Storyboarding the Scene

When it comes to animating on the computer, artists find themselves involved very early in the process. *Monsters, Inc.* as well as all other animated films—whether they are rendered on the computer or produced through cel art—begin with a con-

Graphic designers develop scenes that will ultimately become part of an animated commercial.

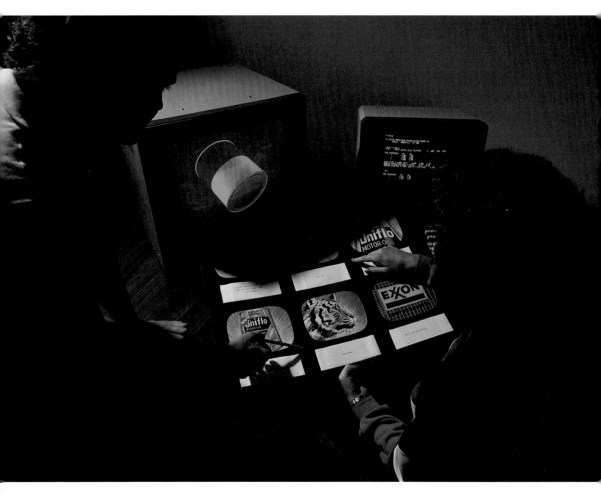

cept, a script, and then a storyboard. Concepts and scripts are typically provided by writers, the people who conceive the story, plot out the action, and compose the dialogue. Storyboarding is the next step. Drawn by artists, storyboards provide the initial visualization for how the films will look.

Storyboards have been used in moviemaking for decades—and not just in animated films. Essentially, an artist is called on to draw the movie, scene by scene, on large poster boards. Storyboards are often rather detailed; their purpose is to give the director an idea of how each scene should be photographed. Working from a storyboard, a director can plot placement of cameras and sound equipment, choose the lenses for the cameras, plan how to light the scene, and decide where to stage the actors. In live-action filmmaking, many directors take a hands-on approach to storyboarding the action because they feel that they are the best judges of how to film the scene.

In computer animation, animators pay strict adherence to what the storyboard tells them to do. The storyboard is very detailed because it will be used to guide the animators in how to render the characters in each scene. In a film that is animated by the computer, one scene must end where the next one begins. Most animated films employ dozens or hundreds of artists working on the movie, all developing different scenes at the same time. Those artists may take months to animate the scenes they have been assigned. If an artist does not strictly follow the storyboard, a choppy scene-to-scene transition may result. Therefore, a storyboard for a computer-animated movie may include thousands of images—one for each camera shot. Patrick Kriwanek, an animation professor at the University of California at Berkeley, explains the process:

> Film storyboards are not graphic novels, and this is an important distinction. The images in graphic novels have no commitment to dovetail from the shot before into the shot after. In film, no shot exists alone; it is a sister to the incoming shot, and must flow into the next shot. It exists as part of a full-motion continuum, and it has to be pre-visualized in that way. . . .

Great storyboard artists understand this, and that is why the boards for *Finding Nemo* or *Toy Story* look exactly like the boards for *Indiana Jones*, because those boards were created by filmmakers, thinking and visualizing the shots in continuity, in service of the greater flow. . . .

The greatest animated films of our time are great because they "feel" like a real movie, they have been constructed by filmmakers using the same guidelines we use to create powerful live-action narratives.[22]

Polygons and Splines

Following the storyboarding phase, the process moves into the computer. The first step in bringing a computer-animated scene to life is known as modeling. The artists who work in this phase of production are known as modelers. Typically, modelers have backgrounds in sculpture or industrial design.

A model is any three-dimensional object—most often a character—that will appear in the scene. Sometimes modeling is done by fashioning a sculpture, known as a maquette, of the character that will later be scanned into the computer. If they choose not to work from maquettes, modelers can work right on the computer, composing a character using one or two methods: polygon modeling or spline modeling.

Polygon modeling is based on a form of industrial design that was developed long before computers started animating films. Polygon design was conceived in 1949 by the architect R. Buckminster Fuller, who used it to design what he called a geodesic dome. A geodesic dome is a sphere constructed by linking together the sides of triangles or similar geometric shapes, known as polygons, each angled slightly. The huge world globe featured at the 1964 World's Fair in New York City and the 180-foot-tall (54.8m) Spaceship Earth attraction at Walt Disney World in Florida are examples of geodesic domes.

Modelers can fashion shapes as complicated as Sully the blue-haired monster by building the characters through poly-

Computer modelers use polygons to build their characters.

gon construction on their computers. Usually, the first step includes scanning a sketch of the character into the computer. Next, the modeler selects points on the scanned image that will provide a general outline of the character. The computer software will then add a series of lines connecting the points. It is similar to making a sculpture out of papier-mâché; in that medium, the artist first constructs a wire skeleton on which the papier-mâché will be applied. Once a computer-animated character's skeleton has been created, the modeler can use the software to fill in the gaps with polygons. For highly detailed work that will show many curves, crevices, corners, wrinkles, bumps, hairs, and assorted other features, the polygons need to be tiny and packed closely together. This process usually takes a very powerful computer, very sophisticated software, and teams of modelers working long hours.

The other method of creating a character on the computer is known as splining. Campers are familiar with splines because they use them as the ribs to support domed tents. Campers first set up the splines, creating a skeleton, then stretch the tent fabric over them. As in polygon modeling, a spline modeler will first scan the drawing, then select the reference points to create the outline and skeleton of the character. Instead of filling in the gaps with polygons, the modeler will use splines. Splining can be accomplished with less-powerful computers than what it takes to produce a model with polygons, but polygons provide a more intricately detailed model. The major animation studios, with multimillion-dollar budgets at their disposal and hundreds of modelers and animators on staff, usually prefer to work with the polygon method.

Rigging

Regardless of whether the artist is working with splines or polygons, the modeler has now created a character in two dimensions. To create a three-dimensional character, other viewpoints of the character must be modeled. For a simple shape, modelers can compose three-dimensional viewpoints by working with additional sketches of the same object. For

A movie artist displays a clay model, or maquette, that was used to build a computer-generated underground city.

example, a modeler can probably compose a three-dimensional image of a bouncing ball by using sketches. This technique may not work for more complex objects or characters; in those cases, the modelers must make use of maquettes. In the large animation studios, modelers will use clay to fashion maquettes of the characters. Maquettes are usually about 14 inches (35.5cm) in length.

The maquettes do not have to be very intricate. Later, the fine details of the characters' faces and bodies can be fine-tuned on the computer. The purpose of the maquette is to provide the reference points for the computer that the modeler can use to fill in with polygons or splines. After the maquette is fashioned, the modeler will typically draw a grid of black lines across its surface. Each place on the maquette where the

RIGGING THE LIPS

In computer animation, one of the jobs for which the rigger is responsible is deciding how to move the lips of the character. This job is particularly important because the lips must move in sync with the dialogue spoken in the sound studio by the actor providing the voice for the character.

To properly rig the lips, the rigger must understand how sounds are formed in the mouth. Each sound is known as a phoneme and requires different muscles in the mouth, tongue, and lips to make the sound. The sound of "m," for example, requires the lips to be pressed together. An "o" sound is made by pressing the cheeks together. Therefore, the rigger must find the places in the lips and face of the character where the mouth can be moved to make the sounds seem natural. Once the lips and face are rigged, the animator runs the character through all the sounds and stores the facial expressions in the computer's memory. Then, when the spoken dialogue is added, the animator can use the appropriate facial expression to match the phoneme uttered by the actor.

Riggers will also look for other places in the face that may move to accompany a sound. They may rig an eyebrow to be raised when a character uses a curious tone, curl a lip if the dialogue requires the character to be sarcastic, or cause lines to appear in the character's forehead if he or she is upset.

An animator has to match the movement of the lips with the words.

lines of the grid intersect creates a reference point. The modeler can then use a handheld scanning device to transmit the reference points to the computer.

The computer now has in its memory every conceivable viewpoint of the maquette. Whenever a viewpoint is called up on the computer monitor, the reference points are filled in with polygons or splines. At this point, the modeler may work for weeks or months refining the images, filling in intricate details, colors, and other features.

The character is now ready for the next step, which is known as rigging. Using the computer, the artist known as the rigger will find places on the character where the image can be manipulated to show motion. Most living things move their bodies at the joints in their arms, legs, necks, backs, feet, hands, and other limbs. Likewise, on the computer, the rigger selects places on the character's body that will serve as joints. To select the joints, the rigger will superimpose a temporary skeleton over the image of the character. When the film is shown in theaters, the audience will never see the skeleton—it will be erased long before the graphics are transferred to film—but it is vital as a tool for showing the animators where the character can bend a leg, crook a finger, or form words with his or her mouth. According to Peter Weishar, professor of animation at New York University, rigging is one of the most important parts of animation because it governs how the character moves. As Weishar explains, how the animator designs the movements of the character is often the most vital task in convincing the audience of the authenticity of the character:

> Even if the character is something as unlikely as a talking giant sloth walking upright on its hind legs, it will be believable if it seems to have weight and presence in the scene. One way to give the character a sense of weight is to "plant" the feet. When the foot is planted it stays in one place until the next step. In CGI the rigger will usually set up a "foot roll" expression that places

a pivot point at the ball of each foot. When the character steps heel to toe, the foot will bend and roll (or pivot) around the ball of the foot. The ball of the foot is then controlled so it stays on the ground until the animator intentionally moves it. This way the character will usually have at least one foot on the ground as it walks, just like in real life.[23]

To do their jobs, riggers often find themselves getting up from their computer terminals and trekking out into the world to study how people, animals, and insects move their bodies. For example, the riggers who worked on the film *Ice Age* spent a lot of time at the zoo studying the motions of big cats so that they could properly plan the movements for Diego, the saber-toothed tiger. Weishar says, "When a tiger takes a simple step, a great deal more happens than just a leg moving forward. His tail may wag a bit, his pelvis will rotate, his back may curve, and various other parts of the body will shift to compensate for the redistribution of weight."[24] Back at their computer terminals, the riggers will use that information to plan how the characters move their bodies.

When an animated character takes a step, there may be a ripple effect on the rest of the body, causing what are known as tears. A tear is the place in the character's body where the polygons stretch too far, causing gaps in the model. If the rigger ignores a tear, the character's movement may look artificial. At this point, the rigger may have to send the image back to the modeler to provide more detail, and therefore more polygons, in the problem areas of the character's body.

Making the Characters Move

When the characters have been properly modeled and rigged, it is time to make them move. This is the actual animation process. Usually, teams of animators will be assigned to each scene. Their job is to bring life to the characters, manipulating their motions through each scene in order to tell the story that has been described in the script and storyboards.

In cel animation, the characters are given motion through a series of drawings, each slightly different than the last. When the cels are run through the camera at a high rate of speed, they fool the eye into believing that the character is alive on the screen. In computer animation, there is no need to provide thousands of images of the character in slightly different poses. Instead, the animator will select a few key poses and then ask the computer to provide the motions of the characters between those poses. To accomplish this task, the animator must tell the computer how much time needs to elapse from pose to pose and which joints in the temporary skeleton must be manipulated. The computer will then move the splines or polygons according to the information it has been fed.

There is no need to produce thousands of cel drawings, but animating through the computer is an incredibly long and tedious process. At Pixar, for example, it has taken as long as five years to animate a single film, calling on the talents of hundreds of modelers, riggers, and animators as well as software engineers and other technical staff members. Sometimes, as in the case of manipulating Sully's 2.3 million hairs, the engineers had to design new software simply for that one task. Weishar says, "There are thousands of details involved in every shot. Whether it is a subtle movement of the eyes, or perhaps a shift in weight that gives the character more presence in a scene, an animator can tweak a single shot for weeks."[25]

At this point, the characters may have been modeled, rigged, and animated, but the movie is far from finished. There are many other components that must be added before the film is ready for the theaters.

Lighting, Backgrounds, and Film

In live-action filmmaking, the sets are usually illuminated by huge lights that shine on the actors. Properly lighting a film set is a craft practiced by skilled tradespeople who must know how

Many steps go into creating animated worlds such as the one that appeared in *Ice Age* (pictured).

to make actors look natural, how to avoid projecting unflattering light, and how to create the mood the director is seeking. In computer animation, the lighting is provided by the animator.

There is a major difference in lighting a live-action film set and lighting a computer animation. To light a film set, the lamps are positioned off set and are shone onto the actors.

Therefore, the lamps themselves do not appear on film—only their light. On an animation screen, the animator cannot shine a computer-generated light onto the characters because that light source would show up on screen. Therefore, the animator must light each character and all other components of the scene by manipulating the color and intensity of each element in the scene. It must all be coordinated so that the lighting appears to be natural. As Carl Ludwig, the head of Blue Sky Studios, which provided the animation for the film *Ice Age*, explains, "Lights really affect a movie's story line. If you use the same type of lighting for the whole movie, it would look boring. You wouldn't be able to tell the difference between a sunny day and a dreary one."[26]

In addition to adjusting the lighting, backgrounds must be composed for all the scenes. In traditional cel animation, an artist would paint a static scene on which the cels are placed and photographed. In computer animation, the background scenes often feature three-dimensional aspects; likewise, the viewpoints shift as the characters move through them. Still, the first step in the process of designing backgrounds requires artists to paint two-dimensional images. These images will help the computer animators design backgrounds, sticking to the concepts for the scenes that have been worked out in advance.

For example, the movie *Ice Age*—which tells of the adventures of a mammoth, a sloth, a saber-toothed tiger, and a squirrel who return a lost human child to his father—required the animators to concoct a barren, prehistoric world. Artists prepared sketches and paintings, which were then refined and scanned into the computer, where they were modeled as though they were characters. Once in the computer, the background artists could choose features from a variety of images—for example, trees, rocks, and cliffs—and combine them into one background. The software used for this process is not that different from the software that enables camera owners to manipulate snapshots on their home computers. Working on the computer, the artists can also adjust colors and other features, such as blurring trees or rocks to help them blend into the landscape.

The final step in the process is to convert the images stored on the computer onto film, which is the only way it can be shown in theaters. In cel animation, a movie camera is aimed at the cels, which are placed in front of the lens and are filmed one frame at a time. Converting computer-animated images to film is a much more intricate process, requiring special equipment that captures the computer's digital images onto 35mm film stock. However, animators do have a role in this process. As the images are recorded on film, the animators can watch the conversion on a monitor and adjust color, light, sharpness, and other features of the images as they are transferred.

Ice Age was released in 2002. Critics declared it a visually stunning example of computer animation. Film critic Roger Ebert contends:

> Few movies have been as painterly as *Ice Age,* which begins with good choices of faces for the characters (note the saber-tooth's underslung jaw and the sloth's outrigger eyes). The landscape is convincing without being realistic, the color palette is harmonious, the character movements include little twists, jiggles, hesitations and hops that create personality. And the animals blossom as personalities. That's because of the artwork, the dialogue and the voice-over work by the actors; the filmmakers have all worked together to really see and love these characters, who are not "cartoon animals" but as quirky and individual as human actors, and more engaging than most.[27]

Learn to Draw

Clearly, producing an animated film on a computer requires many components, including a concept, script, and certainly, the artistic talents of the creators. Tony White, an Academy Award–winning animator and director, points out though that despite all the high-tech gadgetry and techniques involved in

MERGING ART AND SCIENCE AT PIXAR

*A*t most animation studios, the artists have their jobs and the software engineers have theirs, and rarely do the two sides meet. That is not true at Pixar. In recent years the company has made an effort to expose its software designers to the artistic side of the craft of animation. By exposing them to art, the Pixar executives hope to include software designers more in the creative process.

At the company, which is based in Emeryville, California, software designers are encouraged to take lessons in sculpture and figure drawing. In addition, the company's offices are designed so that the employees of the art and engineering departments mingle during the day. "You want their heart here, so you make them creatively satisfied," says John Lasseter, the Pixar vice president who oversees film development.

As a boy, Pixar's president, Edwin Catmull, dreamed of becoming a Disney animator but realized he did not have the artistic ability. But Catmull, who was very good in math, went on to a career in software design. He has headed development of a lot of Pixar's software that provides the three-dimensional element to computer animation. In 1993 his work in three-dimensional animation earned him a special Academy Award. Catmull still harbors ambitions of becoming an animator and has taken sculpture lessons. So far, the only piece of animation he has crafted that has been featured in a movie was a brief three-dimensional scene featuring his own left hand, which was used in the 1976 film *Futureworld*, a sequel to *Westworld*.

Edwin Catmull wanted to be an animator but ended up developing animation software for Pixar.

Quoted in John Horn, "Enough Pixels, Time for Comedy Class," *Newsweek*, April 29, 2002, p. 46.

producing animation on the computer, every computer-animated film starts with an idea, a pencil, and an artist's sketch pad. And he cautions all prospective computer animators that before they learn the complicated software and techniques required to bring characters on the screen to life, they would do well to learn how to draw:

> It is my absolute conviction that to reach an ultimate pinnacle in character animation, you have to study and understand the human figure in all its complexity. Drawing is the foundation that supports this kind of understanding. If you cannot understand a body in structure and movement, then how can you translate its movement in dramatic and meaningful ways?[28]

Animating People

For years, millions of fans have tuned in on Sunday nights to watch the animated antics of *The Simpsons*. The show is a comedy that includes slapstick humor as well as biting social commentary. Although they are fictional animated characters, the Simpsons display plenty of human qualities. Homer, the father, is a compulsive overeater, a lazy underachiever, is not too smart, and is usually a victim of his own rash decisions. Marge, the mother, wants what is best for her family, but she lets others push her around, she can't pass up a bargain, and she tends to clean the house too much. Their son, Bart, growing up to be just like his dad, is the worst student in the fifth grade and seems constantly in trouble.

While the Simpsons display plenty of human foibles, they hardly *look* human. Homer's obesity, Marge's blue beehive hairstyle, the lack of a chin under Bart's upper lip, the yellow color of everyone's skin—these are elements that compose caricatures of people. For most cel animators, characters like the Simpsons are the only humans they have been able to bring to the screen.

Over the years, cel animators have found the human body much too complex to accurately portray on the screen. In the

MATT

As in much of animation, the characters in *The Simpsons* do not look like real people.

few times in which attempts were made to portray people as, well, human, the results have usually fallen well short of perfection. Computer animators have attacked this problem and are starting to show results. Through some highly technical processes—such as the techniques known as motion capture and rotoscoping—the day may soon arrive when an audience sits down in front of a movie screen and won't know the difference between a real-life actor and an animation produced by a computer.

Striving for Realism

People are so used to looking at people that when they see a mannequin in a department store or a doll on a shelf in a toy store, they know right away that it is not a real person. The same rule applies to animation. The image of a human is much too familiar to an audience composed of other humans; therefore, they will not be fooled by what they see on the screen. As a result, animators simply gave up trying and instead elected to portray caricatures of people. Every true cartoon fan knows very well that nobody in real life looks like Bugs Bunny's sawed-off nemesis Yosemite Sam or like roly-poly Fred Flintstone or Popeye, the sailor whose chin and forearms are drawn well out of proportion to the rest of his body. Film critic Steven Levy recalls, "As a kid, I used to watch *Popeye* cartoons every day, and not once did I question whether the animators had 'sold' me on believing that this balloon-jawed spinach gulper was a real person."[29]

One of the places in which cel animators have frequently fallen short in drawing people is in how they depict their movements on screen. People have distinctive ways of walking and using their hands, which animators have found hard to reproduce in cel art. On the other hand, animals, insects, and, certainly, mythological beasts and beings are much easier to animate because audiences are not quite as familiar with their movements. According to film journalist Martin Goodman, "Animals were easier to draw than humans, more fun and audiences seemed far more forgiving of draftsmanship when it came to animating cats, mice and pigs, rather than human beings."[30]

Still, there have been some attempts to portray lifelike people through cel animation. In 1937, after a decade of animating the adventures of Mickey Mouse, the Disney studio produced the film *Snow White and the Seven Dwarfs*. The producers hoped to instill a sense of realism in the film by depicting Snow White and the prince as real-life characters. In Snow White's case, the dancer Marge Champion served as the model for the princess. The animators studied her on film and copied her movements onto their sketch pads. Two years later, the actor Nelson Demorest served as the model for the character of Lemuel Gulliver in another studio's animated version of the book *Gulliver's Travels*. In both films, the human characters mingle among animals, giants, and other mythological figures, making them stand out perhaps too much from the other characters. Goodman says, "Gulliver is a jarring figure, so realistic that he comes off as a special effect in an animated world comprised of far less sophisticated character designs."[31]

But cel animators kept trying. Disney followed up *Snow White and the Seven Dwarfs* with *Cinderella* in 1950, *Alice in Wonderland* in 1951, and *Sleeping Beauty* in 1959; in each case, at least some of the humans were drawn to look human, although there is no question that in each film other characters were drawn as caricatures. Goodman relates, "Disney's films continued to feature human protagonists and typically did not falter in doing so. As realism and naturalism became desirable goals, the human figure was a proving ground for animators."[32] Nevertheless, as well crafted as *Cinderella*, *Alice in Wonderland*, and *Sleeping Beauty* may have been, no animator working on any of those films had the slightest doubt that everyone sitting in the audience would fail to see Cinderella, Alice, and Sleeping Beauty for what they were—cartoon drawings.

Motion Capture

Nearly a half-century later, animators working in both cel art and on the computer were still trying to figure out how to make people look like people. *Toy Story* featured human characters—Andy, the little boy who owns Woody and Buzz; and his friend, Sid, among others—but on screen they did not look like real people either. Meanwhile, game designers were also falling short of developing real-life characters. For example, game critics found Lara Croft just too perfect. "Many a man would be ecstatic if Lara Croft, the gun-toting female lead in the top-selling *Tomb Raider* (game) were a 'real' woman," writes journalist Donna Coco. "Alas, she is not. Lara is one of those characters who falls into the 'exaggerated for gaming purposes' category, with her large chest, tiny waist and shapely legs."[33]

The first major development in improving the look of people in computer animation occurred in 1997, when the producers for California-based game company Activision convinced actor Bruce Willis to serve as the model for a character in an

Animators tried to imitate
the movements of dancer
Marge Champion (right) in
depicting a dancing Snow
White (above).

action and adventure game titled *Apocalypse*. Treating Willis's head as though it were a maquette, modelers drew a grid on Willis's face and scalp and then scanned the points of intersection to create reference points for the computer model. Then, working at the computer, the modelers and riggers were able to create a three-dimensional duplication of Willis's head, which they pasted onto a digitally enhanced body provided by another actor. "Bruce isn't this giant, lumbering guy. He is a strong guy, though. He's muscular but still a believable person. So those type of characteristics we tried to keep in the body—but we pumped

Actors dressed for motion capture, make plays that would take place during a basketball game.

him up a bit with game type proportions,"[34] says Aryeh Richmond, head of Equinoxe Digital Entertainment, the animation company hired by Activision to produce the game.

Willis also provided a few lines of dialogue for his character, Trey Kincaid. Under the original concept for the game, Kincaid was supposed to be a wisecracking sidekick who accompanies the player on his or her mission to unravel a plot that condemns Earth to a series of plagues and wars. But in testing the game, the developers discovered that players would rather assume the role of Kincaid, so they changed the focus of the action to Kincaid's point of view, making Willis the star of the game.

The game developers used another technique to make Kincaid look real. The technique is known as motion capture, or performance capture. It is a process in which the actor's live performance is recorded by digital cameras. The images are then downloaded into the computer, and the animated character is matched up against the live image.

To perform motion capture, the actor must wear a suit containing hundreds of reflective sensors, which are mostly sewn into the joints but also appear elsewhere on the costume. As the actor moves, the camera reads the light reflected by the sensors, thus making a digital record of the actor's motions. To animate *Apocalypse*, the game's producers had Willis go through a number of different motions—running and shooting a gun, for example—recording each motion with the digital camera. Once the images were downloaded into the computer, the animator matched up points on the character's body with the points of light from the costume recorded by the camera. The resulting animation made it appear as though Willis was a game character. Richmond explains:

> We get a lot of nuances (from motion capture) which is especially important when you have the advantage of having someone like Bruce Willis on a project. Bruce carries his weight in a certain way. If you think about it, you can recognize friends by how they move. And when you're dealing with someone we've all seen on a screen larger than life—he is very recognizable—not

just by his looks, but his movements as well. . . . I think you'll see greater and greater use of motion capture.[35]

Filmmakers were also making use of motion-capture techniques. The 2002 film *The Lord of the Rings: The Two Towers* made extensive use of motion capture to animate the character of Gollum, a slippery, evil, elflike creature who leads Frodo on his quest to destroy the ring. Gollum was a CGI character, but he was animated through the use of motion capture. The filmmakers dressed actor Andy Serkis in a motion-capture suit and had him portray Gollum in all of the scenes. Then the filmmakers used motion capture to animate Gollum, matching his motions up perfectly to those made by Serkis. Finally, Gollum was digitally inserted into the movie, although the filmmakers did use Serkis's voice in the final cut of the film.

Animating *The Polar Express*

Although *The Lord of the Rings: The Two Towers* and the other *Lord of the Rings* films are chock-full of CGI effects, the films are essentially live-action movies. In 2004 Hollywood released *The Polar Express*, a computer-animated film made entirely through the motion-capture process. The film was based on a children's book authored in 1985 by writer and illustrator Chris Van Allsburg, which tells the story of a young boy who loses his faith in Santa Claus. On Christmas Eve a magical train, the Polar Express, appears at his home and whisks the boy to the North Pole, where he meets Santa Claus. At the North Pole, the boy finds a huge mechanized factory rather than a quaint storybook workshop where elves make toys by hand. When the boy arrives, Santa selects him to receive the first gift of Christmas—a bright silver bell from Santa's sleigh. To make the film, director Robert Zemeckis elected to use the process of motion capture to animate all of the characters.

Five of the characters, including the train's conductor, a hobo, and Santa Claus, were portrayed by Tom Hanks, who donned the motion-capture suit and performed all five roles in front of a blank screen. Zemeckis points out that acting a role in a motion-

:00:45.29

08:56:18:11 ST.2
SC26A −AA6 , TK09 A

capture suit can be far more difficult than playing a role on the stage in front of an audience. For example, when the part requires the actor to handle a prop, the actor has to go through the motions required in the script without the actual prop in his or her hands. "I believe the only thing Tom missed was having the physical trappings of a costume," says Zemeckis. "He had to remember that the conductor wore glasses when he was the conductor and he had to remember to touch the bill of his cap or adjust his collar, which he would have done more instinctively if he had been actually wearing that wardrobe."[36]

Of course, the animators had a lot more work to do than just create and animate characters based on the movements of Hanks and the other actors. They had to concoct a whole universe of landscapes, backgrounds, and other features for the film that had to appear as real as if they were filmed for a live-action production. In addition, Zemeckis insisted that the look of the film be based on the illustrations Van Allsburg painted for the book. Thus before the first drawings were made for the film, the production company's artists traveled to Van Allsburg's boyhood home in Grand Rapids, Michigan, where they made sketches of the home and neighborhood, which they intended to use for the backgrounds in the film. According to Zemeckis:

In *The Polar Express,* animators modeled the conductor's movements (right) on similar motions modeled by actor Tom Hanks.

The art department explained the very house where Chris Van Allsburg grew up in Grand Rapids, Michigan, was similar to the one depicted in the book. The Polar Express itself is also similar to the kind of electric train set that everybody who was a kid in the 1950s and early 1960s might have had under the Christmas tree. Even Van Allsburg's vision of an industrial North Pole recalled Detroit, which he'd visited as a boy. The story was all resonating from a Midwestern, Middle-American Christmas memory.[37]

Even the costumes worn by the animated characters received special attention by the filmmakers. Ordinarily the animators may be left on their own to concoct the costumes for the animated characters, but in this case the filmmakers called in a Hollywood costume designer, who designed the costumes and then had them sewn and fitted to the actors. Of course, the actors did not wear the costumes during the motion-capture sequences. Instead, the costumes were scanned and their images were downloaded into the computers. They were modeled and rigged and placed on the animated characters.

Production of *The Polar Express* turned out to be a very complicated and expensive undertaking. It took four years and an investment of $170 million to bring the one-hundred-minute movie to the screen. Most film critics applauded the quality of the computer animation, but they also suggested that the filmmakers fell short of producing convincing depictions of humans. Levy says, "While there is much to visually admire in *Polar Express*, the people have a bizarre wax-museum quality."[38] Critic Roger Ebert also thought the animators fell short of duplicating humans, but he still found the characters endearing. He says, "The characters in *Polar Express* don't look real, but they don't look unreal, either; they have a simplified and underlined reality that makes them visually magnetic."[39]

Rotoscoping

Motion capture is a relatively new technology; the first experiments in motion-capture imaging were conducted in the

ANIMATING CLOTHES

*A*nimating clothes has always represented a challenge for computer animators. Whereas cel animators can simply draw clothes onto a character and have them move with the character, that job is far more complicated in computer animation. Usually, the clothes are added after the character is modeled. Therefore the animator has to coordinate the motion of the character with the motion made by the clothing. If the animator is not careful, the character can step out of his or her clothes.

Meanwhile, animators must also be mindful of how clothes move and shift on the bodies of their characters. For example, a character's necktie cannot stay frozen against his body; it has to sway as he walks or flap in the wind if he starts running. A skirt must constantly shift around a character's body. In fact, California-based game animator Thomas Knight says women's skirts are particularly difficult to animate: "Typically, the skirt starts off being tight around her legs. When she walks, you have to morph that skirt so that her legs don't break through the skirt. It's a difficult process."

Quoted in Donna Coco, "Breathing Life into 3D Humans," *Computer Graphics World*, August 1995, p. 40.

1980s. Recently, a much older technology has been updated by computer animators, who are using it to create images of people on the screen. The process is known as rotoscoping, and it was first used in 1914 by animator Max Fleischer. Fleischer built a projector, which he called a rotoscope, to display a filmed image on a screen composed of frosted white glass.

This image shows the stages of creating a cartoon with a rotoscope.

Then he traced over the filmed image, frame by frame, to create a cartoon. The first rotoscoped movie was a film featuring Fleischer's brother, Dave, dressed as a clown. Tracing over the film of his brother, Max Fleischer created the cartoon character Koko the Clown.

Since Fleischer's pioneering work, rotoscoping was used occasionally by animators; in fact, some of the scenes of the prince in *Snow White and the Seven Dwarfs* were rotoscoped. Rotoscoping can be a time-consuming process. Although rotoscoping may work for a cartoon that lasts a few minutes, or to add scenes to a feature-length film, the notion of rotoscoping an entire feature-length animated movie had for years been considered impossible. To produce a ninety-minute rotoscoped movie, filmed at twenty-four frames per second, animators would have to trace nearly 130,000 frames of film. Indeed, it would be a far more difficult task than producing the same number of cels for a feature film. After all, cels depict a single character. For a rotoscoped movie, the entire frame of film would have to be traced and colored.

Even in producing the shorter cartoons, to cut corners the rotoscope animators would skip frames of film. As a result, rotoscoped cartoons often had a choppy look to them because the animators had chosen not to make seamless transitions from frame to frame.

In 2006 animator Richard Linklater revived the rotoscope process to produce the film *Through a Scanner Darkly*. The movie is based on a 1977 book by the late science-fiction writer Philip K. Dick. It tells the story of a detective who must wade into a city's seedy yet mystical drug culture. To produce the animation, Linklater actually filmed a live-action movie starring Keanu Reeves, Robert Downey Jr., and Winona Ryder; then he scanned the film into a digital format. Working on a computer, animators gave the film the look of a graphic novel, which they felt was appropriate given the dark nature of the story. Dick's daughter, Isa Hackett, recalls, "At first I thought the idea of a whole movie done in this graphic novel form was preposterous. But we soon realized that . . . the film's technique was crucial for that feeling of being just a bit, well, off."[40]

The animators on *Through a Scanner Darkly* did not have to rotoscope every frame in the one-hundred-minute film. Instead, like their predecessors, the rotoscope artists duplicated select frames from the filmed version. Those images were scanned into the computer, where the animators made use of software that enabled the computer to fill in the missing frames with altered duplications of the original artwork.

Still, it was far from an overnight job. It took fifty animators a total of five hundred hours for every minute of screen time. Software designer Bob Sabiston, who created the software for the filmmakers, says, "I suppose this is now as sophisticated as tracing can get."[41]

Critics found the film visually stunning. As with Snow White, Trey Kincaid, and the conductor from *The Polar Express*, there was no question that the characters portrayed on screen were not quite human, but they did come close. According to film critic Bob Strauss:

> The convincing detail on the animated actors is just astounding. It sounds like a joke to say that Reeves has rarely given a more compellingly expressed, deeply wounded performance, but in all seriousness, that's what we see here. Downey and Ryder also register some of their best work, and there's not a single supporting character that fails to come off as thoroughly human.[42]

Max Fleischer

Rotoscoping was not the only innovation that pioneering animator Max Fleischer brought to the craft. In 1924 Fleischer unveiled a series of cartoons he called *Song Car-Tunes,* which were the first animations to feature sound. The cartoons told stories that required the audiences to sing along. To help the audience, Fleischer illustrated the song lyrics on the bottom screen and kept time by animating a ball that bounced over each word. Audiences were urged to sing along by following the bouncing ball. Three years later *The Jazz Singer,* starring singer Al Jolson, made its debut as the first film to feature a soundtrack.

Fleischer was born in Austria in 1887 and immigrated to the United States as a young child. After establishing his animation studio, Fleischer produced the first animations of Popeye, Betty Boop, and Superman. In fact, when Superman debuted as an animated character in 1941, Fleischer's cartoons were the first to urge audiences to "Look up in the sky!" The cartoons were also the first to refer to Superman as "faster than a speeding bullet." Fleischer died in 1972.

Max Fleischer, an innovator in animation, works in his studio.

Quoted in Adam Rogers, "The Sorcerer's Apprentice," *Newsweek,* June 22, 1998, p. 84.

Better Left to Humans?

Clearly, animators working with the rotoscope and motion-capture technologies have not quite achieved the effect of duplicating humans on screen. Audiences are not yet fooled by the images they see in animated films; they know they are cartoons. Still, cinema insiders believe the day when the audience will not be able to tell the difference is not too far in the future.

Some critics question whether technology should be heading in that direction. They suggest that there is no need to concoct realistic images of people on the screen. "Why bother when there are plenty of flesh-and-blood thespians who can do wonderful, spontaneous work?" asks Levy. "If we've learned anything in the past half century of digital technology, it's that some stuff is better done with computers. And other stuff is not."[43] Given the rapidly developing pace of technology in computer animation, those are questions filmmakers may soon find themselves facing.

5

The Future of Computer Animation

Computer animation has become part of the popular culture of the twenty-first century. Each year brings dazzling new films and electronic games that push the art of the computer animator to new levels.

There is no question that computer animation will continue to change what people see on the movie screen. For years, filmmakers have been seamlessly dropping CGI characters into live-action films. As the art and science of computer animation improves, filmmakers hope to further blur the lines between animation and live-action movies. Films already in production will feature computer-generated images as more than just minor characters. In the future, CGI characters will be major components of live-action cinema, sharing screen time with living, breathing stars.

But computer animation is no longer confined to the movie screen or the electronic game console. Certainly, computer animation is used to liven up Internet pages. It is also employed as an educational resource. Doctors as well as medical students can learn a lot about the human body by watching computer animations. Consumers can benefit from computer animation. Architects, for example, use animations to give clients virtual tours of their new homes long before the first nail is driven. In the future, as more professionals and businesses find ways to market their products and services through computer animation, consumers are sure to benefit because they will be able to see a virtual picture of what they will be getting for their money.

Finally, when it comes to selling products on television, advertising agencies and their corporate clients have become

A computer model of the human brain can aid doctors and medical students in the study and diagnosis of disease.

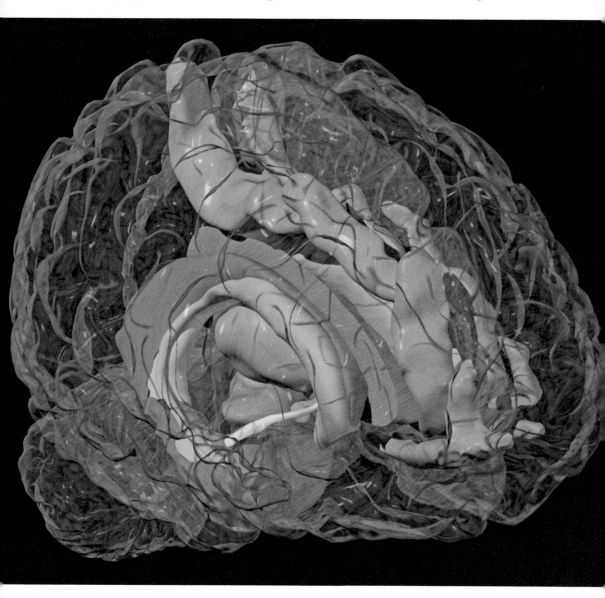

very aware of the effectiveness of computer-animated characters. Anybody who has turned on the television to be greeted by the image of a little green lizard with a British accent is well aware of how well CGI characters can sell products.

The GEICO Gecko

The cockney-voiced lizard, known as the GEICO Gecko, was conceived in 1999 by the Martin Agency, a Virginia-based advertising firm that was employed by GEICO Insurance Company. The agency gave the gecko a British accent and something of a wise-guy attitude, and it has featured the CGI character in dozens of television commercials over the years. The gecko's job is to assure consumers that they will pay less if they buy their insurance from GEICO.

GEICO's investment in the gecko has paid off. In 2004 GEICO's share of the insurance market rose by nearly 15 percent, a better growth for that year than what had been recorded by GEICO's top three competitors, State Farm, Allstate, and Progressive. Each of those insurance companies certainly has its own high-powered ad campaigns, but none has been able to match the gecko's record in boosting market share. In 2006 an annual survey of consumers identified the GEICO Gecko as the fifth most favorite "brand icon" in America. The gecko finished behind the M&M candy characters, Pillsbury Doughboy, the Aflac Insurance Duck, and Tony the Tiger, spokesman for Kellogg cereals. With the exception of Tony the Tiger, all of those icons are computer-animated characters.

In the GEICO commercials, the animators usually place the gecko in situations in which he can interact with actors, whom he counsels to buy GEICO insurance. "He's a lovable character," says Steve Bassett, a Martin Agency executive. "First-graders send in drawings of the gecko. Great-grandmothers do needlepoint pillows of the gecko. Hardly a day goes by when someone doesn't suggest an idea about what the gecko should do next."[44] In fact, as computer-animation techniques have improved, the animators have found that they can place the gecko in most any situation and the audience will pay attention to what he says. "The new gecko is able to sit down and climb things in every conceivable situation," says David Hulin, the gecko's supervising animator. "As always, we want to make sure he performs as naturally and looks as good as he possibly can."[45]

Indeed, other companies have recognized the appeal of computer animation and have taken steps to convert their two-dimensional mascots into three-dimensional characters. In recent years, such familiar corporate mascots as the Morton Salt Girl, the Jolly Green Giant, Mr. Clean, and Mr. Peanut have been reintroduced in computer animation. Other familiar icons of advertising are sure to follow. "It's fun to work on a project where the animated character is immediately recognizable to viewers—like a star," says Jeffrey Dates, creative director for a Dallas-based studio that specializes in producing television commercials. "Of course, since the audience already has expectations of what the star does and looks like, it's a challenge to meet and exceed their expectations."[46]

Architects, Athletes, and Doctors

Essentially, the role of the GEICO Gecko and the other computer-animated corporate mascots is to help consumers make buying decisions. In addition to advertising, there are other ways to market products and services through the use of computer animation.

Architects and interior designers make use of computer animation to provide virtual tours for their clients, showing them how their new homes will look, inside and out, from various angles and points of view. Journalist Dianna Phillips Mahoney writes:

> It's no longer enough, it seems, for architects to present their designs using 2D drawings. . . . Clients, particularly those who may have seen *Toy Story* one too many times, expect more. They've seen or read about

photo-realistic computer generated models; they've seen or read about animated walk-throughs or fly-bys, and they've seen or read about interactive virtual tours through buildings that have yet to be built.[47]

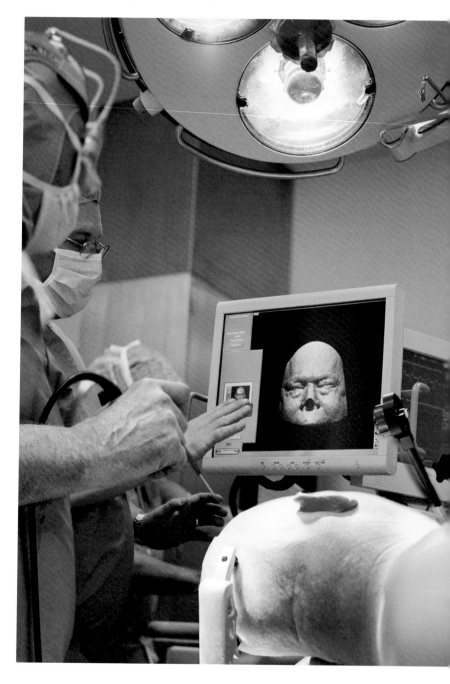

Brain surgeons create a computer model of a patient's head in preparation for an operation.

Modeling an animated home for a client is essentially no different than modeling the ballroom scene in *Beauty and the Beast*. When architects design a project for a client, they often do not have to start from scratch. They may have already stored images of walls, doors, windows, furniture, trees, and other features into their computers' memories. For example, instead of modeling a new door for every room in the house, they can simply drop the images into the animation wherever the plans call for a door.

Large architectural and design firms may employ their own animators. For small, simple projects, some architects and designers may be able to do the animation on their own using hardware and software specifically designed for modest animations. For something more complicated, many architectural and design firms are likely to retain the services of animation studios that specialize in providing architectural animations. "We've found that it takes a team of people to do what we're doing," says Joseph Bayer, president of an Ohio-based animation studio that specializes in architectural work. "We have someone who models, someone who does the actual texturing, lighting and animation paths, and someone else who does the video editing."[48]

In addition to architects and designers, other professionals who can make use of computer animation are physicians and medical students. Some animation studios now specialize in providing animated viewpoints of human anatomy, which may help students recognize the effects that diseases have on organs such as the heart, lungs, and liver. Surgeons faced with tricky operations have made use of animated run-throughs, helping them decide which techniques to employ when they actually cut into their patients. Pharmaceutical companies have commissioned animations to show how their drugs affect areas of the body.

Doctors, physical therapists, and sports trainers have made use of motion-capture technology to determine whether patients recovering from injuries were slowing their recoveries because of the way they walk, run, or use their limbs. One place where motion-capture technology has been used to study sports injuries is Boise State University, which has established a computer-animation studio across the street from the school's football stadium.

Athletes who participate in the program wear motion-capture sensors on their bodies and are filmed running on a treadmill and performing other exercises by six cameras that record light reflected by the sensors. Animators then build models of the athletes in their computers, using their body motions as guides—similar to how Savion Glover was animated for *Happy Feet* and Tom Hanks was animated for *The Polar Express*.

By studying the animations, the Boise State researchers can tell whether a foot injury may be aggravated by the way an athlete lands on the balls of his or her feet or whether pitchers or quarterbacks may be aggravating their shoulder injuries by the way they throw. "There's still a lot we don't know about the factors that contribute to sports injuries," says Michelle Sabick, a biomedical researcher at Boise State. "It's a fascinating field of study."[49]

The Boise State researchers are also using motion-capture animation for more than just diagnosing sports injuries. By studying the motions made by athletes, they hope to give them direction on how to improve their performances. For example, by studying a pitcher's throwing motion—particularly in slow motion—a coach may be able to spot ways in which the pitcher can improve his or her delivery and add velocity to the pitches.

At Boise State, the researchers attached motion-detection reflectors to placekicker David Lowery and instructed him to leap over hurdles. The Boise State researchers believe that by studying the motions of Lowery's feet as they hit the turf, they may be able to provide advice to the football coaches on what size and style cleats to use for different turf and weather conditions. As the benefits of motion-capture animation become more widely known, more sports medicine specialists and coaches will rely on the technology to help improve the performances of athletes.

Forensic Animation

In sports medicine, animation is used as an investigative tool, allowing doctors and therapists to uncover truths about injuries. In recent years, attorneys have also found that computer animation can be used as an investigative tool. They have employed it to simulate car collisions in cases in which drivers who cause accidents have been sued by the victims. The animated simulations show all the important details of the accident, including a depiction of the scene, the weather conditions, the directions the cars were traveling, and other factors that may have caused the collision. Animators take the data provided to them by witnesses and court records and create a brief movie that juries can view to determine guilt and fix monetary damages.

An animated computer reenactment of a crime can help police determine what took place.

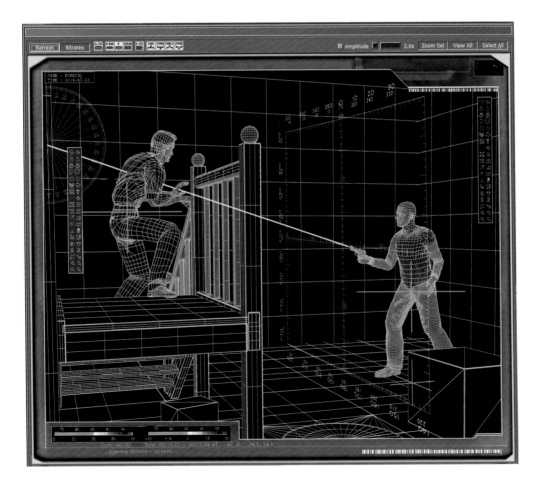

Attorneys are finding so-called forensic animation useful in the courtroom. University of the Pacific law professor Fred Galves says clients should realize that the three- to five-thousand-dollar cost of making a brief computer animation of the accident is worth the cost since monetary damages awarded by juries can total tens of thousands of dollars. "These are animations that win cases," says Galves. "If I was involved in a $50,000 car accident case, I would spend that much money on an animation."[50]

From time to time, computer animations have been used to present evidence in criminal cases. In 1997 prosecutors used a computer animation to provide a simulation of the Alfred P. Murrah Federal Building in Oklahoma City, Oklahoma, which had been devastated by a bomb set by terrorist Timothy McVeigh. The bomb caused the deaths of 168 people, including many children who were in the building's day-care center at the time of the explosion in April 1995. The animation of the building gave the jury a vivid picture of how the facility appeared before it was destroyed by the bomb blast. McVeigh was convicted and executed in 2001.

While the Murrah animation was used to help convict McVeigh, some animations have been used to prove the innocence of defendants. Dena Winkleman, a Connecticut-based animator, was called in by a defense attorney to create a computer animation of a murder. The defendant in the case had confessed to the police, but the defense lawyer believed the confession had been coerced. Working with photographs of the victim, records provided by the medical examiner's office, and other evidence, Winkleman produced an animation that showed the murder could not have been committed the way it had been described in the defendant's confession. "There was no way, judging from the angle and path of the bullet and where it lodged, that the defendant was guilty,"[51] says Winkleman. In this case, the work of the animator helped prove the innocence of an unjustly accused defendant. Certainly, the legal arena is one place where computer animation has the potential to become an important resource.

THE SHEPPARD MURDER CASE

One of the most sensational trials of the twentieth century involved Cleveland, Ohio, physician Sam Sheppard, who was accused of murdering his wife. Sheppard was convicted of the crime in 1954, but twelve years later he won a new trial and was found innocent.

Before he died in 1970, Sheppard insisted the murder was committed by a man hired to wash the windows of his home. In 2000 Sheppard's son, Sam Reese Sheppard, sued the state of Ohio, contending that his father had been wrongfully imprisoned and that the real killer was the window washer. To compensate him for his father's false imprisonment, Sam Reese Sheppard asked for a $2 million payment by the state.

Attorneys representing the state called on computer animators to create a model of the Sheppard home, which had been torn down years earlier. The animators provided a virtual tour of the home, showing the path that would have been taken by the window washer. According to attorney Dean Boland, who represented the state, "We showed jurors the path the window cleaner was supposed to have taken, through a basement window and then right by where Sheppard was supposed to be asleep—in a daybed at the foot of the stairs that led up to the bedroom." The animation also showed how the window washer would have had to return by the same path after committing the murder, again passing Sheppard without waking him up.

Based in part on what they saw in the animation, jurors decided that the window washer could not have been the killer. They ruled in the favor of the state, denying Sheppard's son the $2 million payment.

Quoted in Steven Marks, "Body of Evidence," *Computer Graphics World*, March 2001, p. 48.

Changing Size and Shape

While doctors, physical therapists, attorneys, architects, and consumers will continue to find ways to use computer animation, the major advancements in the field will still be found in cinema and games. It is always difficult to predict how technology will evolve in the years to come, but experts suggest that one of the predominant themes in computer animation will be refining and improving the characters to make them appear even more lifelike than they are now.

In film, one future trend is already unfolding. Movie directors are working on projects that will blur the lines between live-action films and animation. Director James Cameron, known mostly for his 1997 CGI-laden blockbuster *Titanic*, is planning two films that have projected release dates of 2009. The two science-fiction films, *Avatar* and *Battle Angel*, will feature live-action characters but also will use the technology of motion capture to create animated characters who will share the screen with the actors.

Avatar will tell the story of a space traveler and his encounter with alien life-forms. During filming, motion-capture techniques and computer imaging will be employed to immediately convert actors into animated aliens. Therefore the director will be able to look through a viewfinder and watch an actor interact with an animated character, seeing the same image the audience will see in the theater.

It promises to be an enormously helpful tool to the director, who must decide how best to film a story that will be chock-full of CGI effects. In the past, the scene was filmed and the CGI character added afterward by the computer animators. Now, with the computer animators working in real time alongside the director, Cameron can view the scene as it is unfolding. He will be in a position to change the pace of the action, the camera angles, the viewpoint of the audience, and dozens of other features that will affect the action. "It's like a big, powerful game engine," says Cameron. "If I want to fly through space, or change my perspective, I can. I can turn the whole scene into a living miniature and go through it on a 50 to 1 scale. It's pretty exciting."[52]

According to the script, the space traveler is an avatar, or a being that can change size and shape. Cameron says the filmmakers could have used makeup to change the appearance of the character, but CGI will obviously be more effective. "We could put rubber on his face," says Cameron, "but I wasn't interested in doing it that way. With the new tools, we can create a humanoid character that is anything we imagine it to be—beautiful, elegant, powerful, evocative of us, but still with an emotional connection."[53]

Cameron's companion project, *Battle Angel*, will employ similar technology. The film will be based on the exploits of a Japanese comic-book heroine who is part human and part robot. "We're going to blow you to the back wall of the theater in a way you haven't seen for a long time," promises Cameron. "My goal is to rekindle those amazing mystical moments my generation felt when we first saw *2001: A Space Odyssey* or the next generation's *Star Wars*."[54]

While Cameron and other filmmakers look for ways to use computer animation on the screen, electronic-game manufacturers also hope to refine the animation in their products. Better graphics and more detailed images are promised in the future. Also, manufacturers hope to improve the interaction among characters, particularly with how their voices are recorded and replayed during the games. Electronic-game

When CGI was combined with a model of the *Titanic* hitting the iceberg, the effect was terrifyingly realistic.

experts concede that the audio quality of their products has lagged behind the visual quality.

Game animators will also find themselves working in new genres. While action-packed adventures and science-fiction stories have dominated the game market since the days when the MIT students created *Spacewar!*, industry executives cannot help but notice that their customers are growing older. Indeed, most game players are now in their thirties, which means they may not be as interested as they were in the past in saving the world from evil invaders or destroying the cities of their enemies. More mature dramas, comedies, and thought-provoking stories may soon be adapted into electronic games. With such scenarios expected to dominate games during the next few years, animators know they have to improve the voices and other elements that cause the characters to interact with one another. As game developer David Braben explains, "Once you move away from the shooting games, when you are face to face with characters and are not necessarily blowing their brains out, the speech part becomes much more important."[55]

An Unpredictable Future

Computer animation is one of the world's newest art forms—it is still just some forty years old. It is also one of the fastest-changing art forms the world of art has ever witnessed. The computer animations that will appear in *Avatar* will be infinitely more complex, more colorful, and more exciting than the hummingbird animated at Ohio State by Charles Csuri. Certainly, few people who saw Csuri's animation in 1967 could have envisioned the CGI characters that populate movie screens today. As for the types of images that may be produced by computer animators twenty or forty years from now, at this point they may well be beyond the realm of anyone's imagination.

When it comes to the future of computer animation, just about the only guarantees made by experts is that it will be exciting, awe inspiring and, above all else, unpredictable. According to John Canemaker, director of animation at New York University's Tisch School of Arts:

A School for Computer Animators

*M*any high school art departments feature training in computer animation. One school that has taken the lead in training future computer animators is Penn Manor High School in Lancaster, Pennsylvania, where 275 students a year take classes in computer animation, digital photography, and Web page design.

Students who enroll in the animation class write scripts, provide the sketches for their characters, record the voices, and model the characters on the school's computers. By the end of the course, most of the computer animators create short movies that span a few minutes.

Penn Manor's program is regarded as one of the top high school computer-animation programs in the country. Teacher Shawn Canady says, "You watch students come in with a limited ability to represent themselves digitally; and then they (are able to) create amazing graphics—visually rich representations of their imagination."

Quoted in Robyn Meadows, "Making Cutting-Edge Animation; Capitalizing on Teens' Growing Interest in Technology, Video Games, and Art, Penn Manor Begins Offering Computer Animation Classes," *Lancaster New Era*, November 23, 2004, p. 1.

In the future, a new, more expansive definition of "animation" will be required. To create new kinds of imagery, animation will need both to manipulate and merge different technologies, graphics and live action. However, for all the as yet unknowable forms it will take . . . the root meaning of the word will remain apt: animation will always be "the act of imparting life." And as in every art form, the new frontier will be defined not by technology but by ideas.[56]

Notes

Introduction: Why Use a Computer?

1. Rick Lyman, "Computer-Generated Wizardry Is Pummeling Everyone but Disney," *New York Times*, July 24, 2000, p. E-1.
2. John Hayes, "*Happy Feet*: Movie Really Moves Thanks to Stunning Animation," *Pittsburgh Post-Gazette*, November 17, 2006. www.post-gazette.com/pg/06321/739024-120.stm.
3. Quoted in Tony White, *Animation: From Pencils to Pixels*. Burlington, MA: Focal, 2006, p. xv.

Chapter 1: The Computer Takes Over

4. Charles Solomon, *Enchanted Drawings: The History of Animation*. New York: Wings, 1994, p. 40.
5. Solomon, *Enchanted Drawings*, p. 41.
6. Todd McCarthy, "*Return of the King*," *Variety*, December 12, 2005, p. 46.
7. Terrence Masson, *CG 101: A Computer Graphics Industry Reference*. Indianapolis: New Riders, 1999, p. 395.

8. Quoted in Paul Trachtman, "Charles Csuri Is an 'Old Master' in a New Medium," *Smithsonian*, February 1995, p. 56.
9. Charles Champlin, *George Lucas: The Creative Impulse*. New York: Harry N. Abrams, 1997, pp. 51–55.
10. Quoted in Joe Tracy, "An Inside Look at the Original *Beauty and the Beast*," *Digital Media FX Magazine*. www.digitalmediafx.com/Beauty/Features/originalbeauty.html.
11. Roger Ebert, "*Toy Story*," *Chicago Sun-Times*, November 22, 1995. http://rogerebert.suntimes.com/apps/pbcs.dll/article?AID=/19951122/REVIEWS/50208001/1023.

Chapter 2: Games: Computer Animation Comes Home

12. Keith Ferrell, "Quiet on the Set: Interaction!" *Omni*, November 1991, p. 93.
13. Quoted in B.I. Koerner, "How *Pong* Invented Geekdom," *U.S. News & World Report*, December 27, 1999, p. 67.
14. Quoted in David Sheff, *Game Over: How Nintendo Zapped an American Industry, Captured Your Dollars, and*

Enslaved Your Children. New York: Random House, 1993, p. 136.

15. Champlin, *George Lucas*, p. 94.

16. Quoted in Tiscali Games, "Lara's Creator Speaks." www.tiscali.co.uk/games/features/tombraiderlegend.html.

17. Quoted in Donna Coco, "Creating Humans for Games," *Computer Graphics World*, October 1997, p. 26.

18. Quoted in N'Gai Croal and Jane Hughes, "Lara Croft, the Bit Girl," *Newsweek*, November 10, 1997, p. 82.

19. Mike Smith, "Welcome to the Real Next Generation. If You Were Looking for a Critical Reason to Buy an Xbox 360, *Gears of War* Is It," Yahoo Games. http://videogames.yahoo.com/gamereview?cid=1951037562&tab=reviews&page=0&eid=491455.

20. Ferrell, "Quiet on the Set," p. 93.

Chapter 3: Is It Art or Science?

21. Quoted in John Horn, "Enough Pixels, Time for Comedy Class," *Newsweek*, April 29, 2002, p. 46.

22. Patrick Kriwanek, "Storytelling Through Cuts," *Animation Mentor Report*, October 2005. www.animationmentor.com/newsletter.1005/feature_storytelling.html.

23. Peter Weishar, *Blue Sky: The Art of Computer Animation.* New York: Harry N. Abrams, 2002, p. 28.

24. Weishar, *Blue Sky*, p. 29.

25. Weishar, *Blue Sky*, p. 67.

26. Quoted in Jeanna Bryner, "Movie Magic," *Science World*, March 28, 2005, p. 8.

27. Roger Ebert, "*Ice Age*," *Chicago Sun-Times,* March 15, 2002. http://rogerebert.suntimes.com/apps/pbcs.dll/article?AID=/20020315/REVIEWS/203150303/1023.

28. White, *Animation*, p. 286.

Chapter 4: Animating People

29. Steven Levy, "Why Tom Hanks Is Less than Human," *Newsweek*, November 22, 2004, p. 18.

30. Martin Goodman, "Dr. Toon: Running with the Pack," *Animation World*, November 15, 2006. http://mag.awn.com/?article_no=3081.

31. Goodman, "Dr. Toon."

32. Goodman, "Dr. Toon."

33. Coco, "Creating Humans for Games," p. 26.

34. Quoted in Coco, "Creating Humans for Games," p. 26.

35. Quoted in Coco, "Creating Humans for Games," p. 26.

36. Quoted in Julian Phillips, "Performance Capture CGI Techniques Makes '*The Polar Express*' an Advance for Animation," *Skwigly Animation Magazine*, October 27, 2004. www.skwigly.co.uk/magazine/news/article.asp?articleid=346&zoneid=3.

37. Quoted in Mark Cotta Vaz and Steve Starkey, *The Art of "The Polar Express."* San Francisco: Chronicle, 2004, p. 19.

38. Levy, "Why Tom Hanks Is Less than Human," p. 18.

39. Roger Ebert, *The Polar Express*," *Chicago Sun-Times*, November 10, 2004. http://rogerebert.suntimes.com/apps/pbcs.dll/article?AID=/20041109/REVIEWS/41006005.

40. Quoted in Marco R. della Cava, "Through a '*Scanner*' Dazzlingly: Sci-Fi Brought to Graphic Life," *USA Today*, August 2, 2006.

41. Quoted in della Cava, "Through a '*Scanner*' Dazzlingly: Sci-Fi Brought to Graphic Life."

42. Bob Strauss, "Dude, '*Scanner*' Is Just So Wasted," *Los Angeles Daily News*, July 6, 2006. www.dailynews.com/filmreviews/ci_4019929.

43. Levy, "Why Tom Hanks Is Less than Human," p. 18.

Chapter 5: The Future of Computer Animation

44. Quoted in Bob Rayner, "Born Here, GEICO Gecko Goes for Ad-Industry Glory," *Richmond Times-Dispatch*, September 17, 2005.

45. Quoted in Animation World Network, "Framestore NY Gets GEICO Gecko Geared Up Again," March 27, 2007. http://news.awn.com/index.php?ltype=cat&category1=Commercials&newsitem_no=19404.

46. Quoted in Claudia Kienzle, "Animated Pitchmen: They Not Only Help Sell Products, They Create a Lasting Corporate Identity," *Post Magazine*, March 2005.

47. Diana Phillips Mahoney, "Moving Beyond CAD," *Computer Graphics World*, June 1997, p. 20.

48. Quoted in Mahoney, "Moving Beyond CAD," p. 20.

49. Quoted in *Idaho Statesman*, "BSU Professor Studies Sports Injuries," December 17, 2006.

50. Quoted in Steven Marks, "Body of Evidence," *Computer Graphics World*, March 2001, p. 48.

51. Quoted in Marks, "Body of Evidence," p. 48.

52. Quoted in Sharon Waxman, "Computers Join Actors in Hybrids on Screen," *New York Times*, January 9, 2007, p. E-1.

53. Quoted in Waxman, "Computers Join Actors in Hybrids on Screen," p. E-1.

54. Quoted in Anne Thompson, "Cameron Sets Live-Action, CG Epic for 2009," *Hollywood Reporter*, January 9, 2007. www.hollywoodreporter.com/hr/content_display/news/e3i1c5a3d24ccc0c11be93b57ad6f2ed194.

55. Quoted in Mark Ward, "Fast Forward to the Future of Games," *BBC News*, August 30, 2002. http://news.bbc.co.uk/1/hi/technology/2223428.stm.

56. John Canemaker, "Me Tarzan, Me Computer-Assisted," *New York Times*, May 2, 1999, p. A-23.

For Further Reading

Books

Charles Champlin, *George Lucas: The Creative Impulse*. New York: Harry N. Abrams, 1997. The creator of the *Star Wars* series and other CGI blockbusters is profiled in this biography. It includes a chapter on Lucas's work in developing graphics for computer games.

Jeremy Shires, *Careers in Computer Animation*. New York: Rosen, 2001. This work provides students with an overview of the computer-animation industry and suggests ways in which they can prepare themselves for careers as computer animators, such as taking art courses in middle school and high school.

Charles Solomon, *Enchanted Drawings: The History of Animation*. New York: Wings, 1994. Concentrating mostly on cel animation, the book provides a thorough history of the craft, including the work pioneered by Winsor McCay, Max Fleischer, and Walt Disney.

Mark Cotta Vaz and Steve Starkey, *The Art of "The Polar Express."* San Francisco: Chronicle, 2004. Motion-capture technology and other techniques of the computer animator are covered in this book, which chronicles the making of the film.

Peter Weishar, *Blue Sky: The Art of Computer Animation*. New York: Harry N. Abrams, 2002. This book profiles the work of the Blue Sky animation studio, which has produced animations for *Ice Age* and other major films.

Periodicals

Cathy Booth, "Home of the Toys," *Time*, October 18, 1999. The Pixar animation studio is profiled in this article, which provides an overview of how the studio animated *Toy Story* and *Toy Story 2*.

Jeanna Bryner, "Movie Magic," *Science World*, March 28, 2005. This article explains the animation techniques used to produce the film *Robots*.

Steven Levy, "Why Tom Hanks Is Less than Human," *Newsweek*, November 22, 2004. The film critic examines motion-capture technology and whether it succeeds in accurately portraying human movement on screen.

Brent Schlender, "The Man Who Built Pixar's Incredible Innovation Machine," *Fortune*, November 15, 2004. Edwin Catmull, the software designer who has developed many of the important computer-animation technologies used in the film industry, is profiled.

Brent Schlender and Jane Furth, "Steve Jobs' Amazing Movie Adventure," *Fortune*, September 18, 1995. This extensive feature on Pixar explains how the studio grew from a department in George Lucas's special effects company into the dominating force in computer animation.

Paul Trachtman, "Charles Csuri Is an 'Old Master' in a New Medium," *Smithsonian*, February 1995. This article profiles the Ohio State University art professor who produced the first computer-animated cartoon in 1966.

Web Sites

Academy of Interactive Arts and Sciences (www.interactive.org). The academy is the professional trade association of the electronic-game industry. Visitors to the academy's Web site can review the latest developments in game animation and software and read interviews with top game designers. Also, the academy lists the winners of its annual awards, which are presented to animators, software engineers, and other professionals in the field.

Computer Graphics World (www.cgw.com). This site is maintained by *Computer Graphics World* magazine, which covers trends and developments in computer animation. Visitors can read about new developments in the computer-animation industry, view images submitted by top animation students, and read reviews of some of the latest techniques and software available for computer animators.

A Critical History of Computer Graphics and Animation (http://accad.osu.edu/~waynec/history/lessons.html). Ohio State University's College of the Arts maintains this Web site, which provides an extensive history of computer animation, covering the Whirlwind project, the development of *Spacewar!*, the work of Charles Csuri, and the development of CGI for use in cinema.

The Digital Art of Charles Csuri (www.csuri.com). More than four decades after he created the computer-animated cartoon *Hummingbird*, Ohio State University art professor Charles Csuri is still creating art on the computer. Csuri's Web site displays some of his latest creations and also describes many of the computer-animated projects on which he has worked.

Pixar Animation Studios (www.pixar.com). This Web site is maintained by one of the film industry's top computer-animation studios. By following the link for "How We Do It," visitors can study the production of *Monsters, Inc.* through the stages of concept, storyboarding, voice recording, modeling, creating backgrounds, rigging, animating, and lighting.

Index

Picture Credits

Cover: © 2007 photolibrary.com

AP Images, 18, 35, 42, 53

© Blue Sky Studios/Twentieth Century Fox/Bureau L.A. Collection/CORBIS, 58

© Warner Brothers Pictures/Bureau L.A. Collection/CORBIS, 71

© Jerry Cook/CORBIS, 67 (lower)

© Clark Dunbar/CORBIS, 51

© Ralf-Finn Hestoft/CORBIS, 44

© Ed Kashi/CORBIS, 48

© Helen King/CORBIS, 82

© Roger Ressmeyer/CORBIS, 21, 32

© Visuals Unlimited/CORBIS, 79

© William Whitehurst/CORBIS, 85

© Pennington Donald/CORBIS SYGMA, 89

Lucy Nicholson/AFP/Getty Images, 37

Dan Tuffs/Getty Images, 61

Stephen Lovekin/WireImage/ Getty Images, 68

DreamWorks/The Kobal Collection, 13

Lucasfilm/Twentieth Century Fox/The Kobal Collection, 39

Mikrofilm/NFB/The Kobal Collection, 11

Warner Brothers/The Kobal Collection, 9

Belinsky-Yuri/Itar-Tass/Landov, 54

Photofest, 23, 26, 28, 64, 67 (upper), 76

Courtesy of Team Xbox, 45

From *Little Nemo in Slumberland,* So Many Splendid Sundays © 2006 Sunday Press Books, reprinted with permission, 14

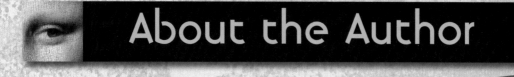

About the Author

Hal Marcovitz has written nearly one hundred books for young readers. His other books in the Eye on Art series include *Surrealism*, *Anime,* and *Art Conservation.* He lives in Chalfont, Pennsylvania, with his wife Gail and daughters Michelle and Ashley.